Joy IN THE MOURNING

Healing From the Death of a Loved One

RUBY (HEPPNER) WIEBE

JOY IN THE MOURNING
Copyright © 2016 by Ruby (Heppner) Wiebe

All rights reserved. Neither this publication nor any part of this publication may be reproduced or transmitted in any form or by any means, electronic or mechanical, including photocopying, recording or any information storage and retrieval system, without permission in writing from the author.

Scripture taken from the New King James Version. Copyright © 1982 by Thomas Nelson, Inc. Used by permission. All rights reserved.

ISBN: 978-1-4866-1292-5

Word Alive Press
131 Cordite Road, Winnipeg, MB R3W 1S1
www.wordalivepress.ca

WORD ALIVE
—P R E S S—

Library and Archives Canada Cataloguing in Publication

Wiebe, Ruby, 1952-, author
    Joy in the mourning : through the valley with the one you love / Ruby (Heppner) Wiebe.

Issued in print and electronic formats.
ISBN 978-1-4866-1292-5 (paperback).--ISBN 978-1-4866-1293-2 (pdf).--
ISBN 978-1-4866-1294-9 (html).--ISBN 978-1-4866-1295-6 (epub)

    1. Wiebe, Ruby, 1952-. 2. Husbands--Death--Psychological aspects.
3. Bereavement--Psychological aspects. 4. Husband and wife. I. Title.

BF575.G7W54 2016   155.9'37   C2016-900580-1
                                                                                                       C2016-900581-X

To all who have walked through the valley with a loved one.

Wherever you are in your journey, may the presence and peace of our Heavenly Father be your constant companion.

Contents

	Acknowledgements	vii
	Introduction	ix
1.	Cancer Knocks – March 1996	1
2.	Cancer Knocks Again – November 2005	6
3.	Reprieve – December 2006 to May 2010	11
4.	Cancer Moves in – May 2010	15
5.	Surgery Again – September 2010	27
6.	Transferred – September 2010	37
7.	Santa Barbara – October 2010	50
8.	Home Again – November 2010	64
9.	Forever Home – January 2011	74
10.	I Choose Life	84
11.	Live to Worship	88
12.	Live With a Plan	91
13.	Live With Purpose	94
14.	Live Reaching Out	98
15.	Live to Bless	102
	Scriptures	105
	Epilogue	107

Acknowledgements

My thanks to my children Scott, Kerri, Berena, and Shalom. You walked that path with me and gave me all your encouragement to write the story.

My good friend, Lois—you inspired me with your own book.

My husband and personal "techie," Larry—I couldn't have done it without your constant help and support.

Word Alive Press, especially Kylee—your patient answers and explanations kept me going when things got overwhelming. And Tom, my faithful editor—your help and encouragement have made the process fun!

Introduction

I've walked through a difficult and challenging time, and I feel it's important to put on paper the feelings I've experienced and insights I've gained. What can be more difficult than standing by helplessly as you watch the love of your life suffer through unspeakable pain? Or what greater challenge than having to say goodbye as he fades away before your eyes? And yet when all is said and done God has brought me into a full life.

I am fulfilled in my daily walk with Him, in my family, friendships, and opportunities to minister with my church family. God has also given me meaningful work that I believe makes a difference in the lives of others. My hope is that at the end of my life it can be said that I walked this road with dignity and class, showing integrity in all my relationships. In the end it is how we treat those made in the image of our Heavenly Father that really defines who we are.

During my most difficult days, I like to open my Bible and read Psalm chapter thirty. I'm reminded there that life goes on and that, after a night of weeping, *"... Joy comes in the morning."* And then I remember how, after the darkest night I ever lived through, joy came in the mourning.

Having said this, I'm tempted to think, "Who wants to read the words of an older lady, hampered by arthritic pain, hair turning grey and who wears too much perfume...?"

I pray that as you read my words you will be encouraged, prepared, and committed for whatever comes to you in life. Difficulties will come, of that we can be sure; my prayer is that you will

Joy in the Mourning

find the strength to become all that you can be and bless others along the way!

Chapter One
CANCER KNOCKS – MARCH 1996

I woke up suddenly at the sound of a thump followed by a soft groan. It was Saturday night, and there was no way I could have known that my life had just changed forever. Reaching over in bed, I realized my husband was missing and I heard him calling my name. He was lying on the floor beside the bed. It was immediately apparent that he was in terrible pain, so I started asking him, "Where does it hurt? Can you walk?"

He had a hard time focusing on my face, but slowly nodded, saying yes to the pain question and no to the other. Larry was a large man—me, not so much. I asked if he could try to crawl to the living room couch. He nodded and proceeded to do so.

About this time our son, Scott, came home from hanging out with friends. He was obviously concerned about the situation and thought we should call 911. Since Larry's pain seemed to focus on the left side, and with a family history of heart issues, we did just that.

When the ambulance arrived after what seemed like an hour's wait (actually only about 10 minutes), I convinced them to let me ride along while Scott followed in the family car.

During the short-long trip to the local hospital, I felt a deep sense of peace and calm that I knew in my heart could only come from having an intimate relationship with Jesus Christ. I could hear my husband praying in the back of the ambulance. The attendant kept asking him what he was saying, but being in intense pain I believe Larry was unable to hear or focus on him.

Finally, I half-turned and said, "He's praying."

Joy in the Mourning

After a short, stunned silence, a quiet "Good" came back.

As soon as Larry entered the emergency unit he was whisked away out of my sight. They had pretty much ruled out a heart attack. After several tests, it was determined that he had passed a kidney clot. Different from a stone, a clot is a miniscule piece of kidney tissue. This of course brought up a whole new set of questions which needed more testing for answers.

They wanted to keep Larry overnight for observation, so Scott and I drove home and finished out the night. The next morning, I had to explain Dad's whereabouts to our three daughters. Since the kids were born, Bible reading, prayer, and church were regular parts of our lives, so it was as natural as breathing to now turn to God, the One who had made us and created us for a purpose. How thankful I was that with our children growing up it was a choice they were making for themselves. In the midst of uncertainty, there was an atmosphere of calm assurance in our home that we belonged to an amazing God and His eye was on us continually and He would care for us no matter what.

After church later that morning, we headed to the hospital to bring Larry home. As he was being discharged, they reminded him of an appointment for an ultrasound the next day. The x-ray he'd had simply showed a deformed left kidney. We had no idea what lay before us, but we were convinced of who our God was and that we were in His hands.

After the ultrasound, a CT scan was set for Friday afternoon. The speedy progression clued us in somewhat that the medical people were taking this seriously. We still had no solid answers, but we were solid in our belief that our God was looking out for us. At home we spoke openly to our children and told them all that was happening. They, too, expressed no fear or apprehension and we had to keep reminding ourselves how blessed we were.

The following Monday we got a call to see the urologist on Wednesday afternoon. They told Larry to be sure to bring his wife

Cancer Knocks – March 1996

along. We realized we were receiving small words of warning preparing us for what we would hear.

I clearly remember sitting in the doctor's office listening to him explain in medical terms that the odd-shaped kidney was evidence that it was literally split apart by a tumor he believed had been growing there for ten or more years.

He looked straight at us and said, "It is malignant."

At that very moment I remember being flooded with an unbelievable peace. As I looked at my husband's face, I knew he was feeling the same thing.

The doctor repeated himself in different words: "You have cancer of the kidney." He seemed puzzled that we weren't falling apart, so went on to explain how he would set up a quick surgery date. With some negotiating, Larry was able to move the date back; he wanted some time to be able to donate his own blood. He also insisted on a repeat CT scan just before the May 17 surgery date. It was March 28, so the doctor complied and we headed home.

The overwhelming peace we had in the office continued. We had been part of a church for several years that encouraged a close relationship with Jesus, and knowing by now the benefits of spending time in God's Word on a daily basis, we could not go back if we had wanted to.

Sharing this news with our children was not something I wanted to do, but it had to be done. Again the faithfulness of our God was evident as they assured us they were not afraid. One by one they each expressed faith in God for healing and His caring. We were so blessed.

Other than the incident that initially took Larry to the Emergency Room, he hadn't ever experienced pain or illness related to the cancer, and he was able to continue working until the day before his surgery.

Joy in the Mourning

Early on the morning of May 17, we headed for St. Boniface Hospital in Winnipeg. We prayed together before leaving the car. When we entered the facility everything was quickly taken out of our hands, but again, we knew whose hands we were really in and we were content. We also had a great deal of confidence in the surgeon, Dr. Deckter.

I spent the next four or five hours in a waiting room praying, talking on the phone, and working on my income tax preparation. In those days I ran a home daycare and because it was my own business, my tax deadline was the middle of June. Thank you, Lord, for small favours. This little bit of downtime gave me the break in a hectic life that I needed to complete this task.

Finally, the doctor appeared and let me know Larry was out of surgery and in the recovery room, and of course what I really wanted to hear, that all went very well and the cancer was contained. They removed it all. Did I feel like celebrating? Well, yes! But honestly, not any more than I had for the past two months.

Eventually they allowed me into the recovery room to see my husband. It was good to see his blue eyes looking back at me and at the same time difficult to see my big strong tower of a man reduced to this weak, wounded shell.

As we continued believing God in the days to come for complete restoration of health and strength, recovery happened much more quickly than predicted. Larry was released to go home on the fifth day after the operation. Two weeks after, he was at his desk at home pricing jobs for his construction business, one week after that supervising on the work site, and six weeks after surgery he was doing the actual work, lifting and all! How we praised God for such a speedy recovery and more even for the fact that he was feeling so well physically!

All the kids at my home daycare loved Uncle Larry so they were quite enthralled when, from time to time, he would show them the "railroad track" a third of the distance around his torso. This track was created by the staples used to close the incision.

Since my husband was self-employed and without insurance beyond what was government issued, there was no income other than what I was able to bring in with my small business. And yet God's hand was evident in the way He took care of us, supplying every need that arose. During Larry's recuperation, a young couple in our church was married. Because we had introduced them several years earlier, they chose us to be their witnesses. What an opportunity to be a blessing. Because of God's provision, we were even able to buy suitable clothing for the honour.

All in all, we looked forward to an awesome future, since the doctor had assured us there was no sign of cancer remaining and no radiation or chemotherapy treatments were necessary. Life was good; our family was growing up and doing well, and we had many years together to look forward to.

Chapter Two
CANCER KNOCKS AGAIN – NOVEMBER 2005

Let me fast-forward nine-and-a-half years. For the first two years after the initial findings and surgery, Larry was required to undergo a CT scan every six months. For the next three years, he had one scan a year. After nine years of enjoying excellent health, he saw our family doctor for a routine annual physical. Since he hadn't had a chest x-ray for a while, the doctor suggested this might be a good time. We waited for the results, thinking nothing of it.

We were quite surprised when the results showed multiple shadows in both lungs. Again, there were absolutely no symptoms pointing to a potential problem. A series of tests and more CT scans followed, taking seven months to reach a conclusive diagnosis. It seemed the test results kept coming back with a one-word response: "Inconclusive." To say we were getting frustrated is a gross understatement! At one point they even thought it was simply an infection he may have picked up in the southern states. Since we had visited south Texas and even crossed briefly into Mexico within the past year, it was a rabbit trail the specialist followed and of course came up empty, again.

One surgeon felt all along that it was renal cancer metastasized to the lungs. However, we were told the only way to know for sure was to do a surgical biopsy, since any other tests and biopsies came back without a certain diagnosis. A date was set and again we knew Larry would be unable to work for some time after, since it was explained they would have to cut through many layers and take out a wedge of his left lung.

Cancer Knocks Again – November 2005

Believing without a doubt that he was in the hands of a loving, caring God, we committed to the procedure and made plans accordingly. I do not want to lead you to believe that we were never frustrated, upset, or downright scared; we were all those things. And yet every time the fear threatened to overtake us even to the point of paralysis, we knew that time spent in the presence of Jesus and meditating on the Word of God dispelled the fear and brought His peace and assurance. Isaiah 26:3 states, *"You will keep him in perfect peace, Whose mind is stayed on You, Because he trusts in You."* It was all about the focus: we could choose to lock our eyes on the fear and all that wasn't right, or we could choose to keep our minds fastened on God and experience His peace. We didn't need to think twice about what to choose.

Again we found ourselves entering the hospital admitting area early on Friday, May 5, 2006. Before my husband was taken to the operating room, he received a visit from a team of physiotherapists to show him some of the moves he would be required to make in the days following surgery. After they left his room he turned to me with a chuckle and said, "They think I won't be starting to move until day three? Watch me!" Again we prayed together, committing him and the entire situation into the hands of our loving Father in Heaven. Then Larry disappeared through the doors separating the OR from the waiting area where I spent the next few hours.

A serious case of impatience was beginning to set in when finally the doctor came. Without preamble he let me know that his suspicions were correct and what he found was renal cancer spread to the lungs. He stopped speaking and looked at me expectantly. I wasn't sure what to say, so I stood there and looked back at him.

He broke the silence. "This is serious."

"Aha," I thought, "he's expecting me to fall apart, and I don't know how."

Aloud I replied, "I realize that, we both do, but we choose to hang onto our faith and hope even as we are aware of the facts. Thank you."

He proceeded to tell me the name of the oncologist he wanted Larry to see as soon as possible. We settled all the details and I was allowed to once again enter the recovery room and observe my strong, manly husband reduced to a helpless shadow of himself.

Being the stubborn man he was, Larry began trying to raise his arm as soon as he was moved into his room. He just had to prove those therapists wrong. True to his word, when they visited late the next day he surprised them by lifting his arm above his head, and all without pain or pulling a staple.

Please let me clarify here that I have no intention of boring you with a lot of facts, figures, or statistics. However, this account is laying the foundation for a lot of feelings felt, lessons learned, and moves made down the road.

When Larry returned home a few days after the procedure, he immediately began making plans to return to work in the near future. Just like ten years before, he had no symptoms nor did he ever experience a sick day due to cancer. Now it was just a matter of recuperating from the surgery, which had turned out to be quite a major affair leaving a deep, long scar.

Whereas ten years earlier we were involved in a wedding soon after his hospital stay, this time we were planning a huge thirtieth wedding anniversary. Somehow the milestone twenty-fifth had slipped past us while our oldest son, newly married at the time, had taken his wife with him on tour in the United States with his band. Our oldest daughter was living in New York, involved in a ministry there. Neither one could be around at the end of May that year, so we put it off for a few years. This was the time. The invitations were out and the venue was secured, but with surgery and missed work again, how would we come up with the extra cash to make it an enjoyable, memorable time for family and

Cancer Knocks Again – November 2005

friends? God is so good and so faithful. Everything worked out and all expenses were paid, again!

Shortly after this celebration, which took place at the end of May, Larry saw his oncologist for the first time. We listened intently as he explained what was happening and what he felt was the best course of treatment. Referring to a CT scan which had taken place after the biopsy, he pointed out the pattern of growth in a matter of a few weeks, and strongly recommended enrolling Larry in a drug trial. Radiation was out of the question, since it was too close to the heart, and surgical removal was not an answer because both lungs were affected. And since there was no chemotherapy known to be effective with this type of cancer, our only option seemed to be a trial drug. Neither of us was comfortable with this, especially after reading four pages of small print listing all the possible side effects. In the end, my husband asked for a second opinion, as we really just did not feel comfortable with this doctor. The specialist told us Larry had three to six months to live if he did not start on a drug immediately. If, on the other hand, he was willing to start right away, he could stretch the time to at least a year and a half.

We decided to insist on a second opinion, because we knew the importance of being in a good, positive frame of mind and having a trusting relationship with our medical advisor. We just weren't feeling it here.

Six weeks later we were sitting in a different oncologist's office. This specialist compared the results of the scans and found no difference—nothing that indicated continued growth. We shared some practical changes we had made regarding diet and alternative measures. There was still no discomfort or symptoms, such as coughing or pressure in the lungs, and Larry was back to work full-time. The doctor was very encouraging and saw no need to push chemical treatment on us. The bottom line for us: we felt comfortable with this doctor and felt he truly cared about us as fellow human beings. How we thanked God for bringing us together, and giving us an incredible peace and assurance in the midst of our circumstances.

By this time we were grandparents. Our son Scott and his wife Renae had blessed us with three beautiful grandchildren: Zachary, Ollie, and Austin! Our second daughter, Berena, with her husband Dean, had just presented us with Maximus, and Rambo and Zeus would follow as time went on. Both of our married children lived near us, as did our oldest and youngest daughters.

Life was good, our family was growing and doing well, and we had many years together to look forward to.

Chapter Three
REPRIEVE – DECEMBER 2006 TO MAY 2010

Life was indeed very good that summer. I soaked it up, having come face to face with the possibility that things can change much too quickly.

It was early November of 2006 when my husband started talking about moving west, and since Calgary was in the middle of an economic boom, it seemed the place to be. It didn't hurt that at the same time Scott and Renae were seriously considering a move there as well. Larry did some searching on the internet and followed up some leads with phone calls; these resulted in promises of unlimited work potential. He would leave on November 22, get established in a job, find a place to live temporarily, and be back home for Christmas. We decided it would be the best for me to stay home in Winnipeg for the time being and keep my daycare running there (I already had several new babies registered to come in, in the next few months). Also our daughter, Kerri, was renting the second floor apartment and Shalom, the youngest, lived at home with us, making it more feasible to keep the family home. So the plan was that this arrangement would probably only last the winter, and with daily flights between the two cities we could enjoy frequent visits.

It turned out that Scott and Renae would be moving to the Calgary area on December 9, and with two vehicles and three very small children, they really wanted an extra driver, so of course I volunteered. Yay! A chance to see hubby!

We left Winnipeg early in the morning with two very loaded vehicles—a car with a standard transmission (which eliminated me as a driver) and a pick-up truck. I spent many hours that day behind the wheel of the truck, which I didn't mind at all, since I find highway driving relaxing and therapeutic.

I remember driving in the dark of early evening with Zachary sleeping in the passenger seat next to me, and it seemed it was just God and me in the entire world. Thinking about our planned living arrangement for the winter months gave me no peace whatsoever. I knew God was showing me His plan was for us to be together; after all, that's why we got married over thirty years ago. It just didn't seem right to continue down this road when we were best friends, and always enjoyed being together, never mind that marriage is hard work at the best of times when you're living together. That's the way God's plan works.

Long before we reached Calgary around midnight, I had settled in my heart that I would be joining my husband in this new location after Christmas. More than a heart settlement, I had cried out to God and told Him I wanted to be where Larry was and if God had shown him this path I would be happy to be there with him. I thought about how I would miss the kids in my care, and how I would miss my daughters and new baby grandson in Winnipeg, but the alternative was unacceptable to me. After all, I would get to spend the winter with the man I loved and my son and his family who were also moving to the same area.

Four days after this life-altering decision, I was flying back to Winnipeg to make last-minute preparations for Christmas and sort and pack up a few things to take along west. We didn't need to take a lot, since we had rented a furnished apartment for the next six months.

It was a bittersweet time. It seems to me that in the depths of my heart I knew even then that I wouldn't be back to Winnipeg to live. Little did I know how thankful I would be a few years down the road that I made the choice to swap the security of a house for the sweetness of a home. When my husband got very sick a couple

Reprieve – December 2006 to May 2010

of years later, I remembered how close I had come to missing out on those months.

Our winter in Calgary was almost like a second honeymoon, right down to living in a small apartment and learning to cook for two again. What am I saying? I never did catch on to that; having grown up youngest of twelve, I had learned to cook for a large crew and couldn't seem to go back.

We were blessed to find a new church family quickly and God brought many wonderful, caring friends into our lives. How we thanked our Heavenly Father for them as the years unfolded. That winter we spent as much time as possible with Scott and Renae and their three sweet children who were growing up much too quickly.

Shortly after our relocation, Larry made a quick trip back to Winnipeg to see his oncologist and run another CT scan. The results came back with no noticeable changes. We were happy for that, but at the same time continued to trust God, our Healer, for total annihilation of cancer in his body. The next step seemed to be finding a new specialist in our new hometown. His doctor in Winnipeg referred him to someone and we made a visit. At this time my husband was still adamant that he did not wish to receive chemotherapy, as he was still only being offered drugs in trial state. His new oncologist was understanding and willing to work with that. She planned on sending him for CT tests at regular intervals to keep an eye on things. We complied with this plan, and since he was still symptom-free other than the spots on his lungs which weren't growing, he was able to work and there was plenty. We also had a great time exploring our new home province and taking advantage of warm, western hospitality.

With time we had the joy of welcoming two of our daughters in their respective moves to Calgary—three down, one to go. I'm still waiting! All this time we were looking for a small town within easy reach of the city to enjoy a quieter, slower pace of life.

Joy in the Mourning

When we found it a few eyebrows were raised. Our new hometown seemed to give new meaning to the phrase wild west! We enjoyed getting to know our new neighbours, and getting involved in community activities.

Life was good, our family was growing, and we had many years together to look forward to.

Chapter Four
CANCER MOVES IN – MAY 2010

As we entered 2010, we had plans for the future regarding retirement in a few years: short-term mission trips, spending more time with our children and grandchildren, and of course extended family. One of Larry's jobs required that he travel to small towns in rural Alberta as a representative for a public relations company. I was blessed to be able to accompany him on these trips. We had an arrangement: I did all of the highway driving while he planned his itinerary for the next town, worked on his computer, or caught up on his sleep. The hours spent together in the car with nowhere else to go gave us opportunity to draw closer together and, of course, became a kind of test of our relationship.

One of these trips was especially telling when I began offering my expert advice on how he could run his business more efficiently. After all, in spite of the blonde hair, I really was quite intelligent and I knew stuff. As you can imagine, that did *not* go over well. We made it through basically unscathed, but when the next trip came up I asked if he still wanted me to come along and he said with a smirk that he would love to have me, as long as I understood one thing:

"If you so much as open your mouth with any advice whatsoever, I will have to push you off the nearest cliff!" Since we were to travel to the Crow's Nest Pass, I realized this was a distinct possibility. I kept my mouth shut and stayed as far from the edge of any cliff as I could.

Joy in the Mourning

On the evening of May 7 when we arrived home from work, Larry decided to walk over to our neighbour's house on the next street to help with a little project. I watched him limp down the road, relieved that he would be seeing our family doctor on Monday to check out the pain that had developed recently in his left thigh. Then I settled down for a little time of relaxation. In the past two months I had been accompanying him on his jobs to Calgary about three days a week and the days seemed to get quite long!

About a half-hour after Larry left the house there was a pounding on the door and my son's voice shouting, "Mom, open up, Dad's been hurt!" Before I could get to the door he burst in and quickly told me how a neighbour had called to tell him they needed me to come and I wasn't answering the phone. The truth was we were using only a cell phone and it was plugged into the charger in our office down the hall; I had heard it ring and with an exasperated sigh decided to let it go to voicemail, wondering why my husband had forgotten to take it again! Guilt shot through me like an arrow as I immediately set out with Scott to see what had happened.

On arrival I rushed over to my husband who was lying on the cold, damp ground writhing and groaning in pain. The first responders were already on the scene, and they told us the ambulance was on its way. I needed to understand what had happened to bring this on, and was told he had simply been standing and talking with the other men there. He had taken a step back to let someone pass and at that moment there was a loud snap and he hit the ground with a scream. One man described his feelings on hearing the sound of the snap in a rather colourful way, declaring it almost gave him a heart attack.

By this time the ambulance was there and I was being questioned concerning any health information I could offer. Of course I disclosed that Larry had a longstanding cancer diagnosis. I also told them about the recent pain in his left thigh, this piece of information being crucial, since it appeared his left femur was possibly broken.

Cancer Moves in – May 2010

There are no words to describe the sinking feeling I experienced at this time. I found myself struggling to catch a deep breath and was immediately assailed with feelings of hopelessness and helplessness.

I find it incredible as I look back and see how, at a time such as this, strength comes. It came, then. How peace surrounds and a deep joy holds us up like a giant inflatable pillow. Peace surrounded, then. At a time when the human brain wants to descend to the deepest depth and drown itself in finality, the human spirit fights to live! Mine fought. Now take that human spirit and fill it with the presence of the Holy Spirit, the one who created me for an abundant life in Him. How does that happen? I can only call it a miracle and give the glory to God.

Scott and I followed the ambulance to our local hospital and, after a short wait for x-rays, we were informed that Larry had, indeed, suffered a spiral fracture to the left femur. They had no way of treating such a serious injury in a small county hospital, so he would be taken to a facility in Calgary. Although I had suspected this would happen, this knowledge brought a sinking feeling knowing that once there I would be left on my own because my family would need to resume their lives. By now Scott had notified our pastor and we knew our church family would be praying. I felt buoyed up by that inflatable pillow again.

Our youngest daughter had moved back to Winnipeg for a short time and we let her and her sister know what was going on, as well as putting a quick call through to the oldest, who still lived in Calgary. It was one of the most difficult conversations I had with all of them. I hated to have to relay news of this kind to our children. I also knew that every one of them had a relationship with God through Jesus Christ and that they would be carried on their faith and trust in Him. Somehow no matter how old they get, they are still our children and our deepest desire is to protect them from anything hurtful.

Joy in the Mourning

Arriving at the Peter Lougheed Hospital some time later, I was impatient to see my husband, but was told to remain in the waiting room until they had him stabilized. It seemed like hours but in reality may have been one. I was at one of the lowest points ever in my life. Looking back now, I can't help but wonder why I felt more helpless at that time than even at his eventual passing. I can only conclude it was because I felt blindsided! Life had been going smoothly and now we were suddenly hit with this. We had plans to get a lot done that summer. We had the sketches prepared to build a sizeable addition to our mobile home, and between two part-time jobs financial provision was assured. It seems rather superficial to be thinking of finances at a time such as this, but there it was: the realities of life were pressing down on me and there I sat, all alone! Larry, who would have been the first to remind me that God was the source of our supply, was in no condition to speak and I had nowhere to turn but to that source Himself. Somehow I could imagine my loving Heavenly Father sitting me on His lap, placing His loving arms around me, and assuring me that just as He'd promised in His Word, *"... my God shall supply all your need according to His riches in glory by Christ Jesus"* (Philippians 4:19). He could not go back on His Word.

Called to the examining room, I walked down the long corridor with that promise resonating in my brain. I could still feel the presence of my Lord walking alongside me. Right then and there I knew beyond the shadow of a doubt that this was the way it would be—Jesus and I walking this journey together—and fear left me. I would like to say I never again struggled with doubt, fear, or unpleasantness. Negative thoughts attacked me many times in the next eight months but then, in that moment, my choice was made to trust God's promise, not just for provision but for health, strength, and the courage to face head-on whatever lay before us. What a privilege to be able to make that choice knowing that every resource I needed to stand behind it was mine.

Cancer Moves in – May 2010

As I entered the tiny cubicle where my husband lay in excruciating pain, my knees nearly buckled. A nurse was working with him and I asked when he could be seen by a doctor. It seemed there would be a wait, so as soon as we were alone I went to his side, took his hand, and began to pray over him. Immediately the atmosphere became lighter and Larry even said the pain was becoming more bearable. We sat together silently after that, I'm sure each of us lost in thoughts, praying the doctor would come quickly and order immediate corrective surgery.

We did not have long to wait. However, instead of surgery plans the doctor said they would be admitting him as soon as a room became available and we would probably have to wait until the next day, because they needed a CT scan to determine if we were dealing with cancer.

Ever since the leg pain had appeared three weeks earlier, we had both been thinking about a possible recurrence of cancer. Neither of us had shared our secret thoughts with the other. Several years earlier we had done some research on renal cancer and found that it was likely to spread to the lungs, bones, or the brain. For four years it had been present in his lungs—not growing nor shrinking, just there. In spite of the prognosis four years before, he lived a good healthy life, with lots of energy for a man nearing his sixtieth birthday, and never ill. We had been very blessed. We had made many lifestyle changes—diet, exercise, stress relief, etc. Larry had even been seeing a homeopathic doctor for the past two years, and we felt she'd had a huge positive impact on his life.

Now, again, we made the choice to leave our burdens with the God who had made him, created him for a purpose, and held us both in His loving hands. In leaving the care with Him, we also chose to walk away with God's peace and joy. There was that inflatable pillow again.

In just minutes a young lady from the physiotherapy department had arrived to put his leg in traction for the sake of comfort.

Joy in the Mourning

This proved to be a very painful process. I had to leave the room, as I could not stand to see Larry in that kind of pain. I thought to myself, "I better just learn to suck it up and face it; this is just the beginning." Almost as quickly as I re-entered the room, she was finished.

The waiting game continued, but not for long. Soon another nurse entered and told us Larry was to be admitted to a ward upstairs, and the traction would be removed for the transition. I felt awful for Larry, thinking of the pain this would cause him again.

He was taken upstairs and put into a regular bed, heavily sedated, and settled down for what we both hoped would be a few hours of sleep. Having been up early Friday morning, worked all day, and now enduring severe physical trauma, my husband needed the rest. I sat up in a chair near his bed and tried to get a little sleep myself. I did manage to doze a little, but gave up after a while, found a restroom, and tried to prepare for the day ahead by making myself look somewhat presentable.

It proved to be a long day since nothing, not even morphine, seemed to touch the pain. I wished beyond anything that I could take the agony for him, but all I could do was watch and pray. This, I did. In between, I spent many hours on the phone with our children and siblings, his and mine. We continually reminded each other that we were in the care of a loving God; if His eye is on the sparrow, a lowly little bird, we knew we were not beyond His view. Just knowing this kept us going, and our hearts hurt for those who don't have the kind of relationship with Jesus that gives such peace and joy.

Eventually they took Larry down for a CT scan, and we didn't wait long for the report. The surgeon came to his room and told us that, just as they suspected, there was a malignant tumor at the top of his left femur and it had been eating away his bone, weakening it and causing pain for some time. Because of the tumor, they would have to do a procedure before the surgery to set his leg. This was to cut off the blood supply to the growth, eliminating the potential for heavy bleeding during surgery. After the procedure there would

Cancer Moves in – May 2010

be a limited window of time for the operation. It was late Saturday afternoon and they could not proceed until the next day. We hated to think about waiting any longer, but we had no choice, so I decided to go home for the night and get a proper rest. My daughter, Kerri, was planning to go with me and I dreaded leaving Larry for the night. Worse than that, I dreaded telling him I was leaving.

As I suspected, Larry was distraught at the thought of my departure, but as I explained to him, I also had been up at the crack of dawn the day before and worked all day, and other than the few winks I had caught while sitting upright in a chair, had been basically sleepless for thirty-six hours. I could tell he was struggling to understand, but most of all he was just struggling. I knew he was receiving good care and if I didn't get some sleep I would be no good to him the next day, already being at the point of near-collapse and starting to feel ill. Rest and sleep was what I needed and it was time to take care of myself. With a heavy, aching heart, I left his room and promised to be back as soon as possible in the morning.

The next morning I re-entered Larry's room feeling rested and ready to face the day. He, however, had not rested well; they were trying different pain medications, which were causing him to hallucinate. We both knew we were at the end of our resources, emotionally and physically. At the same time we knew we were being held up in prayer by many people—friends, family, and any connections that came out of that. Right now, in fact, we were assured that our church family was standing with us and we were so grateful. It was Sunday morning, May 9, Mother's Day to be exact. Also, many of the extended family we had spoken with had spread the need for prayer to their respective church families; we were covered!

A little before noon, Larry was taken out of the room for the pre-surgery procedure and I was told the actual operation would take place later that afternoon. Some of the family had joined me and we were all relieved at the prospect of getting this day behind us so our husband and father could begin the recovery process and hopefully the pain would be reduced. It was almost forty-eight hours after breaking his femur, and it was yet to be set properly with a rod and pins.

Needless to say I spent most of the afternoon in waiting, on the telephone. Both of us were from large families so I found it most efficient to have one liaison in each family that would be responsible to pass on any information. We were both so incredibly thankful for our families and their support in every way.

With joy and relief, I made contact in the early evening to report a successful surgery behind us. The surgeon had joined us in Larry's room, explaining what he had done and encouraging us with the news that we could start the recovery process. He felt that by the next day Larry would be able to stand, putting weight on his right leg only, since the bone on the left needed to fuse before it could bear weight.

I left for the night a little later with a lighter heart, looking forward to seeing my husband the next day and watching him move forward. After two full days in limbo, it almost felt like we could get on with life again. We clung to our faith in a God who knows what we are facing and will carry us through anything, over any hurdle, and bring us safely to the finish line. We chose His joy and peace, committing each other into His hands as we prayed together before I left.

How good it was to enter the next morning and see a man who was getting his spirit back in spite of an almost sleepless night. The pain medications they were trying were causing huge problems and we concluded he should probably go on to the more conventional post-op painkiller, Tylenol 3. I was still sneaking in his homeopathic medicines, some of which were for pain control. I say sneaking because this is literally what I had to do. This practice would not have been looked on favourably by medical staff. However, the cocktail we chose worked just fine and in a few days he was feeling so good he was begging to be released. With the

Cancer Moves in – May 2010

help of physiotherapy, Larry was learning to walk with crutches and do all the things he would have to do for himself when he got home. Who knew he needed lessons on how to dress himself after all these years.

If you remember, his first surgery to remove the initial tumor had been on May 17. The second surgery, the lung biopsy, took place May 5. This latest operation just happened to be on May 9. We joked that we would be tearing the May page out of the calendar each year.

With promises to follow doctor's orders closely, I was allowed to take my husband home on Saturday, eight days after the accident, six days after surgery. With a much lighter heart than I'd had for a week, I drove him home, stopping to pick up prescriptions and a few homecare aids. If felt wonderful to bring Larry into our home and settle him down, making him as comfortable as I could. Things were already looking up, and we anticipated a good recovery and, if not always smooth, at least an improvement in health as we fought to annihilate cancer.

We began to settle into life again, as regular a life as we could, and things were going well. We had been planning a trip to Manitoba to attend Larry's family reunion the last weekend of June, and we felt he just might be ready by then. Of course, there was the financial cost to consider. With no income and a lot of outgo, extra travelling for medical reasons, and extra costs involved with the illness as well as general living expenses, we knew our resources would not last long.

We chose to bring our needs before God, thanking Him for caring for us and providing all our needs. We had always been faithful in tithing and giving to every need God put on our hearts; we were not about to stop now. You see, we had come to understand this truth from God's Word:

Give, and it will be given to you: good measure, pressed down, shaken together, and running over will be put into your bosom. For with the same measure that you use, it will be measured back to you.

—Luke 6:38

We committed ourselves to stand firmly on this promise and, like Peter when he walked on the water to Jesus, remain focused on Him, the answer to our every need. I would like to tell you it was that easy and we never hit a snag in our faith, but like Peter there were many times in the months to come that we began to sink because our focus slipped from Jesus to our circumstances. At these times the Word of God we had hidden in our hearts came to life, breathing new faith into our pontoons, buoying us up and moving us on. Psalm 37:25 states, *"I have been young and now am old [or healthy and now am ill]; Yet I have not seen the righteous forsaken, Nor his seed begging bread."* Taking these promises, we stood on verses found in Hebrews 10:35–36: *"Therefore do not cast away your confidence, which has great reward. For you have need of endurance, so that after you have done the will of God, you may receive the promise."*

God began to speak to us in this vein. If we don't have enough to meet our need, what we have should become our seed. Just like it would be foolish for a farmer to use up all his seed for food, we realized it would be foolish for us to use up the last few dollars in our bank account to pay a partial bill when we felt God was asking us to trust Him completely, and truly we were at a place where we didn't have a choice anyway. I'm happy to say obedience won out as we cheerfully gave what we had, shoveling out with our little teaspoon (which was only half-full) and watching God begin to shovel back into our lives with His huge front-end loader!

God began to put us on people's hearts. I don't know how, I don't know why, except that I fully believe that when we take

Cancer Moves in – May 2010

God at His Word and place our trust in Him, He does what He has promised: take care of His children (Mathew 6:33–34). There was never a month when our needs were not met and every bill paid. Even our trip to Manitoba for the family reunion was provided to us! And of course we never failed to return to the Lord a tithe of the gifts that came our way; we also remembered to thank God for people who heard from Him and acted in obedience. We prayed God's blessing over them and believed with all our hearts that their lives would be enriched because of what they had done for us.

I can't describe how good it felt to be together at home, beginning the process of recuperation and spending time together in the Word, strengthening our faith. I believe it was a season in which both of us came face to face with the reality of our wedding vows: in sickness and in health.

Each morning Larry woke up feeling a little less pain and a little more hopeful. Each day, I grew into my role a little more, learning how to care for the needs of a grown-up unable to do for himself. Yes, he had been attacked by cancer twice before and yes, he had endured several related surgeries, but he had always been able to walk before and his recoveries had been relatively quick and easy. This time I found myself having to take on a lot of the day-to-day tasks my husband had always protected me from. I'm blushing as I say this, but I had no idea how to go about paying the bills. It wasn't that I had been kept in the dark. We always discussed financial matters and he was good at communicating our financial status to me, but this was just one of the jobs he always did. I learned quickly. And I survived! I also learned how to deal with car maintenance, since our car chose that summer to wear out the front end and then decide she needed new tires. What's a girl to do? Larry did well in advising from the sidelines and guiding the decision-making, but the hour-long drive to the shop for repairs was mine alone and again, I survived. God is so good.

Joy in the Mourning

We felt with the surgery behind us and the hope of new bone fusing around the rod in Larry's leg, we had a lot to look forward to. Life was good, we knew God was on our side, and the future was bright with His promises.

Chapter Five
SURGERY AGAIN – SEPTEMBER 2010

It was Father's Day and Larry's sister Irma and her husband Bill had come up from Virginia to visit. We enjoyed a few days together, and then it was time to leave for Manitoba and the huge family reunion my husband's brother had worked so hard to pull off. As I mentioned, we had been blessed with a financial gift to attend this event. We started out with Bill and Irma, and after the first couple of hours driving we met up with other family who took our American relatives with them and we were left to continue on our own. We did not even try to drive straight through as we usually did, but rather took two days to make the journey to Winnipeg. This was alright, since I was the only one driving. Larry was feeling well enough to make the trip, although it did take a lot out of him.

I am astounded, now, at our audacity. To even think of taking a trip like that with the challenges we faced every day just getting him up and ready for the day, not to mention getting through the day and then getting him settled comfortably for the night. At home this was often the time for me to get caught up on everything I couldn't finish earlier. Being a goal-oriented, list-driven person, I found it difficult to settle in the evening if everything wasn't caught up. Of course, now some things were non-negotiable. Certain tasks just could not be left for the next day. Now I think about it and often wish I had taken more quiet times in the evening with my husband, reflecting and engaging in encouraging conversation. However, I determined years ago that I would not set up my tent in the swamp of regret but rather remember long enough to let it change how I move forward.

Driving those many miles and long hours gave Larry and me opportunity for meaningful conversation. When health is suddenly challenged as his was, it seems meaningful becomes more than a byword. We truly engaged more in important conversation, activities that served to bind us together more closely and time spent in prayer reaffirming our faith in God and His promises. Life and time on this earth became more precious.

The family reunion was good in the sense that it gave Larry that one day of connecting with his siblings and nieces and nephews for what I believe we all felt might be the last time. It was that day when he suffered a severe setback. In preparation for the weekend, his brother had planned for him to ride a lawnmower to get around the grounds more freely. When Larry started to drive it, the clutch sprang back and caused something to snap in his right leg high up in his thigh. It was the left side that had been fractured earlier and had a rod and pins inserted. He had been told he could do normal activities using his right leg only. Now he was almost completely immobile. Somehow we made it through the rest of the weekend and Larry was even able to move around with crutches a little, putting some weight on his right side.

We headed back home on Monday not knowing the extent of the damage to my husband's body, but several months later a CT scan revealed that he had very little of his right hip left, and the pelvic bone was also steadily disappearing. We were astonished to think that while it was apparently "safe" to bear weight on his right side, it was obviously not a good idea.

After that trip, I noticed a definite shift in Larry. His positive attitude was slipping. The pain level intensified, and he had to go to stronger painkillers, which brought many negative side effects.

His brother suggested Larry should try drinking a little red wine every day to help with his digestion. My husband had never been a drinker; rarely had his lips tasted wine. So we became regulars at the local liquor outlets. Then when the pain became

Surgery Again – September 2010

unbearable and prescription drugs were not able to touch it, he fell further off the wagon. How ironic that this straight-laced, clean-living Christian man was now becoming a regular imbiber, scheming how and where he could get his hands on some marijuana. We had a few chuckles over that!

It turned out our son knew a kid who knew a kid, so one Friday evening at dusk we parked our car in a deserted lot by the river and waited. After some time a car drove up and parked about fifty feet away. A young, skinny kid wearing a hoodie walked over and stuck his hand in the driver's side window. I quickly took the small baggie and handed him the required bills, and breathed a hugely exaggerated sigh of relief as we drove on home.

That was the only "buy" we ever participated in. After certain friends found out about Larry's new painkiller of choice, they began bringing gifts. God is so good and faithful. As our pastor said by way of encouragement, "If God created it, it was for good and for our use. Just because some people abuse it doesn't mean it's a bad thing." I concur!

As the summer continued, Larry became weaker and weaker to the point where we became preoccupied with trying to keep him comfortable. He had continued to decline any kind of chemical treatment, and none of the pain medications he had been using seemed effective. The most trying times for me were when my big, strong husband, the one I was in the habit of leaning on, was forced to tears by intense pain on a daily basis! At those times, I would leave the room as soon as he was settled and indulge in a crying jag of my own. When all the crying was done and we both returned to a few minutes of sanity, we were able to remind each other that God had not forsaken us and we chose to stand on His promises and move on.

Larry began to talk about seeking help in an alternative treatment centre in the United States, several of which he had researched online. After some discussion, we put that thought on the backburner for a few reasons—the most glaring, of course, being financial. We continued from day to day doing what needed to be done and trying to keep the pain at bay.

I cannot forget to give honourable mention to our son Scott, his wife Renae, and their three wonderful children. They were an incredible support to us that entire year. Because they lived very close to us, they were there to lend a hand and encouragement every day, often just to stay with Dad so I would be free to go out and run a few errands.

The day came when we had to make the drive to Calgary for Larry's follow-up x-ray, to check on the femur through which they had inserted the rod in his leg. On the drive down we spent some time in prayer, again committing ourselves into God's loving hands and accepting His promises as ours. By the time we arrived at Peter Lougheed Hospital, our spirits were up and we knew that no matter what, our God was with us and He would never leave or forsake us.

Within the next hour it was evident to us that the bone was not fusing as we had hoped, but rather was being eaten away by the cancer. A moment of deep disappointment, and then we were reminded of whose we were, and we began reminding each other of the promises we had read just that morning in the scriptures. Until you find yourself in a similar situation, that may sound like a lot of religious clichés. When you are the one whose life hangs in the balance, you suddenly find you must choose whether to give in to despair and sink into depression or tie a knot in the rope of trust and peace and hang on for dear life. We chose the latter.

One small note of hope given us that day was that the surgeon mentioned a colleague in another hospital who was successful in building synthetic bones. He was willing to refer my husband for a consult. We were eager to take him up on it, so an appointment was made for three weeks later. We returned home that day with hope in our hearts, thanking God for turning the situation around once again.

Surgery Again – September 2010

Larry was no longer able to use crutches, spending all his waking moments in a wheelchair. This meant every time we went anywhere I helped him transfer from chair to car and back again. As well, I was doing all the driving and upon reaching our destinations I was the one to handle the chair, collapsing it and storing it in the trunk for the drive. I'd like to say it kept me fit, and maybe at first it did, but it also wore me out to the point where it was getting very difficult to complete this little task. My dear brother-in-law helped me figure out how I could just roll the chair into the back seat, eliminating the hoisting of a heavy weight. How I thank God for looking after all these little things that made a big difference.

By the middle of August that summer, Scott had built us a wheelchair ramp and made our lives a lot easier and stress-free. We waited for the new surgeon consult with great anticipation, and August 26 found us entering Foothills Hospital with hope in our hearts. The visit left us with a positive outlook, although realizing there were no guarantees. We listened carefully as the doctor explained how he would go about building a new bone, and then said Larry would be able to put weight on his left leg immediately after surgery. If we had been a little more ignorant, that may have put a smile on our faces, however we knew that after not using his left leg for four months he would need some serious physiotherapy before he could actually walk on that leg. The date we were given for surgery was about a week away, which came as a pleasant surprise. We have all heard much about long wait times for surgery and related medical tests, so this was encouraging news.

A week later, we entered the hospital again in an upbeat frame of mind, looking forward to an operation the next day that would give my husband his legs back and me my husband back. This first day was going to be filled with blood work and various tests. We had a time of praying together and I left to take care of some errands. It was so exciting to think that tomorrow the worst would be over. Larry would have to work hard to regain strength in his legs, but we looked forward to his release from hospital and getting on with our lives.

Life was great, we were so blessed, and with our God on our side we were looking forward to many good years together.

Later that afternoon, I was in my husband's hospital room when the doctor entered and the expression on his face said the news wasn't good. The calcium level in Larry's blood was much too high to safely consider surgery. Because of the disintegration of his bones, calcium was building up in his system and, had they proceeded with the surgery, the chances of suffering a massive heart attack on the operating table were high.

Then the doctor asked about Larry's current brain function, concentration, and memory. We smiled and made a light comment like "Aren't all men somewhat brain-damaged?"

He chuckled with us momentarily, and then turned very serious as I went on to explain that I had noticed difficulty in that area. Larry had been experiencing difficulty hearing for several years already, but recently when he asked me to repeat myself I would look right at him and raise my voice, and he still had a puzzled look on his face as if he hadn't understood and then needed a minute to process before he could respond. I had put it down to high pain level and medications. Now it made perfectly good sense that he was just having a hard time focusing and processing his thoughts. Another area was difficulty in making phone calls. When he wanted to call his brother, for instance, he had the phone number in front of him and still didn't seem sure of how to punch in the numbers.

We began to understand what was going on, and it had nothing to do with his ability to hear. The answer to this was an IV flush, which would use a medication to release the excess calcium from his system, since the body does not naturally do this. The plan was to begin the intravenous intervention immediately, and hopefully proceed with the surgery on Tuesday, just four days later than the original plan.

Surgery Again – September 2010

By Monday morning I noticed a distinct difference in Larry's level of thought clarity and responses, and I was encouraged. The most recent blood work also revealed a major decline in the calcium level, so he was deemed a good candidate for surgery once more. That afternoon he had to undergo an angioplasty, a procedure in which a balloon was inserted into a major artery in his thigh to block the supply of blood to the tumor in his leg, eliminating the risk of excessive bleeding during the operation. After this procedure, they would have a window of less than forty-eight hours to complete the surgery. The procedure was successful, but left Larry in such severe pain it was virtually uncontrollable. It seemed nothing could touch the pain and his suffering was difficult to watch. I remember feeling utterly helpless and able to do nothing but pray as I continually adjusted and re-adjusted his legs and the pillow under them. I have a vague memory of doing nothing but that for six days straight. I seemed to be living in a daze, and at the same time thanking God that I was able to be there for him. What I was going through was nothing compared with what Larry had to endure.

On Thursday of that week, Larry's sister Irma arrived from Virginia. Her trip had been planned to coincide with his discharge from the hospital so she could help me out at the house for a few days. Of course now she had to visit him in the hospital as we were still waiting for surgery. Until he was stabilized, there was to be no operation. By Thursday evening the pain level was down to normal and our hopes began to rise. The forty-eight-hour window had passed, but the procedure could be redone at any time.

By morning we knew that, again, it would not be happening anytime soon.

Early in the morning before I left for the hospital, the phone calls started. I could tell the man on the other end was not my husband, although the voice was his. Then my son called and asked what was wrong with his dad. Scott had been receiving calls throughout the night and morning with paranoiac demands and tales of trauma. When I arrived at the medical centre it was to news that new blood work showed a severe imbalance in his electrolytes. Surgery could be a fatal step if that wasn't stabilized first.

It hit me then that my husband, the man I had loved for thirty-five years, who had always been my rock, was in a very vulnerable position. The possibility not making it through the Labor Day weekend was very real. I called our children, three of whom were living in Winnipeg, and they all chose to come for the weekend. It was a bittersweet reunion. We could not leave his bedside for a moment; he did not grasp where he was, why he was there, or why he was kept tied down. The paranoia took over and we constantly had to intervene to avoid having his lines and tubes pulled out. I believe with all my heart that the only thing that kept me sane in those days was staying in the shelter of the wings of an Almighty God. Keeping my husband committed into His capable hands and singing or listening to worship songs was my life, and became the very air I breathed in the months to come. God is good; He was good then and He still is now.

By the beginning of the new week, things were beginning to turn around. The man I knew to be my husband was returning to me, his blood work was returning to normal, and things were settling down. Our daughters had all returned to their home province and our eyes were once again focused on the upcoming life-changing surgery. On Thursday, Larry was once again submitted to the angioplasty procedure, this time with more positive outcome. The pain afterward was at a believable standard and all calcium and electrolytes were at acceptable levels. The operation to give him back his legs would go forward on Friday, two weeks later than originally scheduled.

By this time, Irma had returned to her home in the south and would not be able to help out when we got home, but I was okay

Surgery Again – September 2010

with that since we had a good, broad support base in our friends, family, and church.

The morning of the rescheduled surgery dawned clear and beautiful, a perfect September day. We were both in good spirits, feeling very positive about what was taking place that day. As I said good morning and prayed a short prayer committing Larry and the surgeons into God's capable hands, my heart filled with joyful anticipation.

I spent the next couple of hours on the phone catching the family up on the latest news, stopping occasionally to say a brief prayer. I needed those moments for my own strength as much as the man on the operating table needed it. The entire summer, I had been recording all the verses I could find in the Bible that spoke of strength. Every day I felt such an incredible drain on my own human strength, there was no way I could humanly do everything that needed doing. I had found that by acknowledging the presence of the Holy Spirit in my life and allowing His fruits of love, joy, and peace just to *be* in my life, and be inserted in every activity and every task, it truly brought a level of supernatural strength I would never have known otherwise. Even now when I think of the verse, *"The Joy of the Lord is [my] Strength"* (Nehemiah 8:10b), I experience the exhilaration of being back there and living the moments again, knowing with experiential knowledge that God's Word is true and His promises stand the test—any test.

It seemed like hours, and it was, before I received word that the surgery was over and it was successful!

I cannot express the excitement and anticipation I felt as I practically ran down the hospital corridor to see my husband in the recovery room. I was welcome to visit Larry briefly, as he was still under intense observation. We exchanged broad smiles as I stopped by the side of his stretcher, although his smile had a rather sleepy quality! It was *so* good to see him, and see his smile. The last words from the surgeon before he disappeared into the operating room had been that we could still anticipate some complications simply related to the level of calcium in his system—heart failure being the most suspect. After a quick kiss and assurance that many of our family and friends were praying for his quick recovery, I had to leave and wait for Larry to be moved back to his room.

Later that afternoon back in Larry's room, we talked a bit about the future, and determined to keep up a positive outlook. We both knew this was essential to a great recovery as well as an outlet for expression of our faith, so we focused on plans for his return home. We spoke of possible locations for the physical rehabilitation he would need to bring back his left leg. We also talked about the celebration we would throw for family and friends when the most challenging part of this journey was behind us. We could not have known it would be a year before that party became a reality. Nor that when it did, I would be the only one left to do the planning, and instead of Larry being the master chef manning the barbecue, it would be a couple of men from our church kind enough to step into the gap. The party's theme would also change from a celebration to a way of saying, "Thank you for helping us through the most difficult year anyone could imagine living through."

Finally the long-awaited surgery was over and we could look forward to a bright future. As my husband was always quick to remind me, "The best is yet to come!" And we definitely looked forward to the time ahead being better than it had for the past few months. Things were looking up and our children and extended families stood with us as we anticipated many great years together, although we were all aware that the immediate future did present many challenges. God is good and has a hope and a future in mind for us, according to Jeremiah 29:11. We had so much to be thankful for and so much to look forward to!

Chapter Six
TRANSFERRED – SEPTEMBER 2010

Something had been nagging at me for a while based on a statement made by the doctor. He had maintained that as soon as the operation was over, Larry would be able to put weight on his left leg, and with physiotherapy he should be able to walk again. I couldn't help but wonder how that was possible, since he hadn't been able to stand on that leg for months and his muscle tone was lost by now. However, we hoped for the best. When several therapists showed up in his hospital room the following week, they explained that therapy would only be started after he was transferred to a rural hospital. We were then given several options, each of which would bring my husband closer to our home and make it possible for me to move back home and visit him daily. One particular hospital stood out to us as having a good physiotherapy program, and that is how he came to be transferred to Didsbury Hospital.

Larry had for some time been experiencing pain in his right knee, and he kept mentioning it to anyone who came into the room—doctors, nurses, social workers, etc. Finally, his primary doctor ordered a CT scan. The scan took place on Monday, three days after his surgery. By the following morning we were given the results: his right hip was virtually gone, eaten away by cancer, and about half of the pelvic bone was also missing. What he felt in his knee was deferred pain, we were told. The doctor's instructions were to keep weight off the right side and only stand with his left leg. But of course, with no muscle tone, that would not be happening any time soon.

As we were left alone to digest this latest bit of information, our thoughts went back a few months to the day of the family reunion. Larry had suffered an injury of some sort when the clutch of that riding mower popped back, jolting his right leg backwards. The excruciating pain then, and the long-term effects now, seemed to indicate that those bones had already been compromised at the time of the accident. Up to that point, he had seemed to be recovering from leg surgery. After that day, his body began a descent he couldn't seem to pull out of.

Plans went ahead for his transfer to Didsbury. I was looking forward to getting my husband to a smaller hospital, where I felt he might get more rest and get started on some therapy. Of course, I also looked forward to leaving behind my daily treks across Calgary. The drive to Didsbury would take the same amount of time, but without rush-hour traffic to deal with.

On Thursday afternoon, the transfer took place by ambulance. I followed in my car, going straight to the hospital to make sure Larry was settled in and comfortable before I left for home. Before saying goodbye, we took some time to talk about what was happening. We were still, on some level, trying to digest the latest prognosis. We were told that Larry was now in a palliative state, which meant the medical help received would focus on keeping him as comfortable as possible.

As believers in God and all His promises, we chose to cling to His words of healing, strength, and peace. We were determined not to let Satan and circumstances steal our joy, and we spent a few minutes in prayer together to recommit ourselves to standing in faith.

Arriving at home that evening was definitely a bittersweet experience for me. I was happy to be home after three weeks of living out of a suitcase at my niece Debbie's house! On the other hand, it was a lonely place to be without my husband of almost thirty-five years. Little did I know.

Transferred – September 2010

The next morning, I was anxious to get to the hospital and see how Larry's night had been. It was certainly a relief to be able to drive down the quiet country highway and enjoy the beautiful colours of autumn, listening to the birdsong reaching my ears through closed car windows. This in itself was inspiring compared to the three-coloured traffic lights and honking horns by impatient drivers. It brought joy and an excited anticipation to my heart. I couldn't help but thank God for His precious gifts, given freely on a daily basis.

When I entered Larry's room, he, too, was exhibiting a more relaxed countenance than I had seen on him in some time. I was so encouraged. Outward circumstances had not changed, but the peace of God was tangible in our hearts and in that hospital room. We knew what Jesus had said in John 10:10. He had come to give us abundant life, and we were determined to take that life and live it joyfully as long as God gave us breath to do so.

I would like to tell you that all was well from that time on, and that physiotherapy was successful, but that would not be accurate. In reality, we came to feel that a few of the staff members were treating my husband unkindly and had to be reported. Neither of us wanted to have to deal with this; it took more emotional energy than we had to spare. Out of necessity, and for the sake of the other patients, it had to be done.

The therapy we had been hoping to get was not carried out after all, because of his fragile condition and the fear of causing his bones to crumble further. As a palliative patient, my husband was not viewed as a viable candidate anyway; he was not expected to live more than a few months at most.

During Larry's first week in Didsbury, we got a phone call one day from our youngest daughter, Shalom, who had recently moved to Toronto. She said, "Can I come home now?" Of course the answer was, "Yes, yes, yes!" I knew I desperately needed her company and emotional, moral support! She arrived about a week later and it was so good to have her close. It seemed she was a little surprised at how ill her dad really was.

Shalom had already gone online and secured a job interview for a position in our small town of about four hundred. That there was a job available was in itself a miracle. Shortly after arriving home, she had the interview and landed the job. We were all very thankful that she would have something to keep her mind and hands occupied, and as well be able to support herself.

Besides Shalom, Scott and Renae with their children visited the hospital frequently. I tended to make the trip every morning, trying to arrive by nine o'clock. I would spend the day doing most of Larry's care; it seemed the staff was so busy in this small facility they were relieved to be freed somewhat from the responsibility. The heart-wrenching time came every evening around eight when I prepared to leave. How he hated to be left alone! I began to understand that he truly was left alone, since according to my husband his calls for help were often neglected. I realized, though, they were extremely short-staffed during the night shift. In my heart of hearts, I cried every time I left his side at the end of a long day. I had to hold my tears so I wouldn't add another burden to his heart. I was determined to be strong for him, because he had no strength of his own left. The dam usually held till we'd had a time of prayer together and said goodnight. I would drive out of the parking lot with tears running down my cheeks, hampering my vision. At times like this I knew there was only One who understood what I was feeling, only One who could bring comfort to my breaking heart.

I'm always amazed at what a difference a good night's sleep can make in my attitude and outlook on life in general. Every night I would enter my home thoroughly exhausted from caring for my husband. Before sleep I would again verbally hold him up to my loving, caring God, committing him to the Lord who loves us more than anyone. The thought was never far from my heart that

Transferred – September 2010

I may have just said goodnight for the last time, may never receive another kiss from the love of my life. There was always the issue with high calcium in his system. As his bones disintegrated, the calcium had no place to go. One of the negative side effects was how it would affect his heart. Massive heart failure was a very real possibility. I tried not to dwell on that, and that effort proved to be a daily, or shall I say nightly, challenge.

It was Friday, September 24, and in the middle of the afternoon we received a visitor. She introduced herself as the palliative care nurse assigned to Larry. She was not employed in the hospital, but rather made the rounds within the county. She had come to share with us some of the issues and challenges we would be facing in the weeks to come, as well as to give us lots of materials pointing us to various resources. It suddenly occurred to me to ask if I could bring him home on weekend passes. She was very much in favour, and immediately sprang into action setting everything in place so I could take him home that day on a two-day pass. Within two hours, all of his medications were ready to go and all signatures on paper. I was so happy, so excited, and so scared.

On the drive home, we talked about what we could expect during his brief stay. I was envisioning a quiet, restful time, during which I could devote myself to keeping him as comfortable as possible. He was talking about going camping! We compromised and went to the nearby campground on the Little Red Deer River on Saturday evening for a bonfire, hot dogs, and toasted marshmallows. What made it the most memorable time was that Shalom was able to join us, and Scott and Renae came with their three delightful, fun-filled children! We so enjoyed that evening, the only dark spot being that our daughters Kerri and Berena with her family were unable to join us, since they were two provinces away. We always knew that in their hearts they were with us and would have been with us in the flesh had it been possible. Their dad and

I understood they could not disrupt their lives in that way, nor did we expect it of them. It was a wonderful weekend.

With a heavy heart, I returned my husband to the care of the hospital staff on Sunday afternoon. The next morning, I went directly to the nurse's station to share an idea and seek their input. The weekend had gone so well that I was hoping we could make it a regular event. The staff was agreeable to the idea, but made it clear that in the future they would need more than an hour of preparation. It seemed everything had just worked out for us and they were as surprised as we were when it happened so quickly. Of course, I assured them we understood and would comply. And, by the way, we wanted to work towards bringing him home permanently. That got their attention! In response to that bombshell, we received an afternoon visit from the head of the homecare department. She outlined the steps we needed to take and made an appointment for a home visit. This was necessary to determine whether our home would accommodate my husband with his present physical limitations, and to see what changes needed to be made, if any.

Several days later, the homecare coordinator came to our house for an assessment. Very little needed to be done to get ready. I assured her our son, Scott, would be able to take care of anything I was unable to handle. He had already shown himself quite capable in building a wheelchair ramp earlier in the summer. One doorway needed to be enlarged to accommodate a wheelchair, and a few items purchased or rented to aid in my husband's care. Beyond that, we were good to go as soon as they could get the paperwork done. I shared the good news with Larry as soon as I arrived in his room later that day. We were both very encouraged in looking forward to the move that we felt would free up a lot of time I was now spending on the road.

About this time, Larry was scheduled for another x-ray, for which he had to be transported to Foothills Medical Centre in

Transferred – September 2010

Calgary. I drove myself to the hospital so I could be with him for the test. Just a block from FMC was a Tim Hortons restaurant and as I drove towards the medical centre I thought I should pick up a coffee and his favourite snack: a toasted cinnamon raisin bagel with strawberry cream cheese. All the times we worked together in the city, I couldn't recall a time when he ordered anything else. So I met my husband in the x-ray department with my hands full and he was thrilled. I guess you could say he didn't get out much; not in those days.

Just a few days later, we were told it might be possible for Larry to have another surgery to rebuild his hips and pelvic bones; however, he would first be required to have at least one radiation treatment to speed up healing of his leg. Until this time, Larry had steadfastly refused any chemo drug trials, and radiation had not yet been offered. He thought about it for a while and decided it was worth a try. Again he made a trip by ambulance to Tom Baker Cancer Centre in Calgary. Again I met him there, bringing Shalom with me this time. The radiation proved too much, and he became very ill, causing the procedure to be aborted. One more trip to the Tom Baker Centre was needed for us to hear from a team of surgeons that Larry was too weak to tolerate another surgery and there was nothing more they could do. We had already heard this weeks before, and yet they had come back to us with another possible solution. We felt like our emotions were being batted around like a ping-pong ball. We believed in the healing power of God and we spoke it, daily expressing our faith in Him. At the same time, we were both feeling quite battered by the storm raging in our circumstances, and we spent many moments just crying in pain—emotional pain for me, and emotional as well as physical for my husband. However, we always came back to what and who our faith was based on in the first place. Many well-meaning Christians, friends and family alike, were cautioning us not to hang onto false hope. The way I see it, the phrase "false hope" is an oxymoron, since there is nothing false or negative about hope! Hope is never a bad thing; it keeps me going when nothing else can, it picks up my spirits when everything inside me says "Give up!" and of course, what really makes the difference is the object of my hope. I choose to put my hope in the God who created me and gave me a divine purpose to live in this day, at this time. Not only has He ordained me to take my place in this life, but He empowers me to fulfill His purpose in everything He calls me to do.

Thanksgiving weekend was approaching and we were making plans for another two-day getaway from the hospital. This time we gave ample notice and were on schedule to leave Friday afternoon. I got a major surprise that morning when Larry announced to me that he was still hoping to be able to go to an alternative cancer clinic in the south. Immediately my mind came up with all the reasons why that couldn't happen. Luckily, my brain engaged before my mouth went into gear. In very short order, I heard the quiet voice of Holy Spirit caution me about becoming negative in the face of Larry's deep desire that he had mentioned months before. Now, I asked him to tell me about it: exactly what he wanted, what he would like to accomplish, and how he felt we should go about it. After listening to him, I was able to share my feelings and reservations. First and foremost, I felt that God was not limited in His ability to heal my husband right there on the spot—without having to spend weeks away from home in his compromised condition, and without the high price tag attached, when we had no way of meeting those financial obligations on our own. We also needed to consider the prognosis; we had been told my husband had only a couple of months to live. I assured him I had no time or energy left to do any fundraising, so unless someone else offered to do it, that left only himself. He insisted that he wanted to try, and I felt God impressing on me that I had to support him in this. Larry had always been a strong leader in our home and I knew that even in the midst of illness I needed to let him continue in his God-given role.

Transferred – September 2010

As soon as we arrived home that afternoon, Larry was on the phone calling clinics in the United States. He had narrowed his choices to two, and after speaking to the director of each, it became clear to him. Considering the one in Santa Barbara, California, had an opening in two weeks made it a relatively easy decision. Money was not an issue, since we had nothing to put into it! Our daily and monthly living was dependent only on God and how He went about putting us on the hearts of many friends and family members. We prayed every day, thanking God for those He was using to meet our needs, and asking that He bless them and return an abundant harvest back to them. Now Larry took the responsibility of raising extra funds! For me it was an especially difficult time. Swallowed pride does *not* taste good. That entire weekend, while my husband was at home and on the phone with people we knew, I constantly gave it all to my loving Heavenly Father. I committed every facet of this endeavor to Him, knowing that if we ended up not going, God was still in it. Either way, He had a way.

It was a busy weekend, with three of my siblings and their spouses coming for lunch on Saturday, and Larry's dear nephew arriving late afternoon for a quick fly-in visit from another province. Sunday, our kids living near us all came for a traditional Thanksgiving dinner. In an effort to convince myself things were as normal as they could possibly be, I really wanted to do this. Of course, we missed those who were absent incredibly. Our girls living in Manitoba often expressed their feelings of helplessness, wishing there was more they could do. We understood, both that they were too far away to be able to help in all the practical ways, and also that they would feel that way and why. We were so very thankful for the support of our son, Scott, and his wife. As well as for our daughter, Shalom, who was living in our home for the time being. Having Scott and Renae live so close had its other perks: grandchildren who could pop in any time and give their smiles, hugs, and kisses! We both treasured those times and their grandpa especially appreciated seeing them. During one of these visits, Zachary told us he had asked Jesus to come into his heart. Another time shortly after, Ollie told us she "put Jesus" in her heart. I believe hearing this from his grandchildren gave Grandpa a boost.

By the time I returned Larry to the hospital on Monday afternoon, we had committed to making the trip to Santa Barbara, trusting that God would provide for the clinical treatments as well as our living expenses while there. More than half of the necessary funds were already in, and Shalom had offered her services in setting up flights and accommodations. As well, she had taken time off from her job to accompany us on the trip down. I, especially, was very thankful for this. Just trying to keep my husband comfortable and as pain-free as possible seemed a full-time responsibility. The added stress of looking after logistics would have weighed much too heavily on us both.

We had already spoken to the doctor about the possibility of going away for alternative treatment, but now we had a definite plan with a date in mind. On Tuesday we let him know, and we chose the following Monday as a discharge day. He felt they could have everything set in place by then and final blood work completed. It was very important for Larry to undergo an intravenous flush to help eliminate the calcium build-up in his system. This flush needed to take place about every two weeks at this time, and the plan was to continue them as long as they were still effective. Although we did notice the time between flushes getting shorter, and of course this was concerning and became a serious matter of prayer. We knew to watch for certain signs and symptoms, and those were always followed up with a blood test to determine the necessity of a flush.

It seemed everything kicked into high gear that week. There were a few little things to get done at the house to prepare it for Larry's homecoming. By the weekend, the house was ready and

Transferred – September 2010

all needed supplies and personal care aids were purchased, rented, or borrowed and we looked forward to bringing our husband and father home where he belonged.

Monday, October 18, was a beautiful autumn day. As we drove into town, Larry had me stop at the local polling station so he could go in and vote. It was Election Day.

It was good to move my husband back into our home. Except for two weekend passes, he hadn't been home for almost two months.

Arrangements were made with the Issels treatment centre, flight reservations were made, and accommodations secured. I had the remainder of the week to think about packing everything we might need for a one-month stay, besides taking care of Larry and most of his personal needs. Of course, it was nothing like getting ready for a vacation. I was dreading the trip and the time we would have to spend there. The unknown loomed large in my mind, and while this whole endeavor brought hope to our sagging spirits, it also became an extra drain on our physical and emotional resources. Larry looked forward to the time at the clinic with great anticipation. I feel even now that in a way his mind was cushioned, numbed somewhat by pain, medication, and calcium overload, to the point where the real-life challenges of what we were about to do didn't touch him. Looking back, I'm relieved that he was spared. To my daughter and me, just getting on the plane without further injury to my husband was becoming a big deal.

As the week progressed, the toxins were building up in Larry's body and each day the pain grew more unbearable. We called on everyone we knew for prayer, specifically for a release of toxin build-up to eliminate a large portion of the pain. October 23, Saturday, was the day of departure and on Wednesday Larry was unable to sit up for more than a few minutes. Three days later he would be expected to be up in a seated position for at least eight to ten hours. We needed a miracle just to get him to Santa Barbara. We believe in miracles and were expecting one. Sometimes it would be nice, though, if God would just send one down right now. Why wait till the last minute?

During that week before we left, we were able to again administer some "natural painkiller" by lacing pancakes with the potent stuff. This seemed to bring Larry more relief than anything else, but we knew we would not be able to sneak it across the border, nor did we want to try. We came up with a plan: he would get up at 6:30 on Saturday morning and eat a quarter of a pancake. Then at 8:30, after arriving at the airport, I would feed him another quarter, being very careful not to touch it with my hands and leave the telltale residue. We were confident this would work and together with prayer and our wonder-working God, we were going to make it.

Friday, my poor husband was unable to move himself from the bed to wheelchair. As he cried in pain, I had to leave the room or break down in front of him, and I desperately wanted to be strong for him. I would like to be able to say I was a tower of faith for him to lean on and pull his strength from. Unfortunately, many times I left the room and in my heart cried out to God to take my dear husband to Himself and out of the constant pain and anguish. Shalom and I often shared these thoughts with each other, crying in desperation and guilt for even thinking it. As I watched Larry struggle, I chose to just focus on what God's word says about healing and His desire concerning healing for His children. I called a few friends and family members to stand with us in agreement for release and alleviation of pain.

After lunch that Friday, Larry insisted on getting into the wheelchair and being moved to the living room for a practice run. "After all, tomorrow I have to be up all day!" He was able to get into the chair and I wheeled him to the living room. By the time we got there, he was begging to go back to bed. I complied. And

Transferred – September 2010

I cried. We had tried everything, but there was nothing moving, and again we prayed together, believing God for release. Just minutes after our prayer, Larry asked me to bring the commode. I did, and then left him for a while.

We were able to celebrate later, as we recognized nothing short of a miracle. That evening, Scott and his family came over. Larry sat up in his chair in the living room and chatted the whole time. He was so excited and hopeful. We finally got him settled down for sleep. The morning was coming early and he needed to conserve his energy.

Saturday morning, we put our pain control plan into action. We got to the airport in good time in spite of the dense fog. The hour-long drive was filled with upbeat chatter and verbal rehearsal of our plans for the day. Larry and I waited inside the terminal while Shalom took the car to long-term parking. I took a plastic baggie out of my handbag and, holding the contents with my hand on the outside of the bag, I fed the small morsel to my husband, putting it directly into his mouth. I threw out the bag and cleaned my hands. Then we prayed for a quick, smooth transition from point A to point B, and to point C, and so on throughout the day. By this time Shalom was back and we were able to go through U.S. Customs. Again we felt the hand of God as we proceeded from one thing to another. Everything went smoothly and in due time we were seated on the plane awaiting takeoff. At the scheduled time, we began to move and pick up speed and again our hopes lifted and took flight as the wheels left the runway.

Chapter Seven
SANTA BARBARA – OCTOBER 2010

The contrast in climate hit us the moment we exited LAX airport—from a chilly, foggy morning in Calgary to a hot Saturday afternoon in Los Angeles. So far Larry was taking the trip very well and as we waited for the shuttle bus to Santa Barbara, we just enjoyed breathing in the warm air and letting the sun's rays chase away the northern chill.

The city was oh-so-busy, and we were again relieved to leave the travel details to Shalom. We followed her lead and watched for the right bus to come along, waiting half an hour. The bus was wheelchair-fitted and the seats were comfortable, so we were able to transfer Larry to a seat. Sometimes just a change of position or padding would bring a measure of comfort.

The two-hour bus trip along the scenic coastal highway brought much-needed distraction. It was a beautiful day, warm and sunny, and our spirits lifted as we sped along. Back home we had debated taking a small commuter plane to Santa Barbara, but because of the longer wait for another flight and knowing smaller planes are more crowded and almost impossible to get Larry to a seat, we had chosen the more spacious shuttle bus. Now I was thankful we had really thought through the process. The ride, although longer, was smooth and comfortable.

The bus made only a few stops in Santa Barbara, so we made sure we got the stop closest to the hotel. "Almost there," I thought as we called for a cab. In a short time our ride appeared and we loaded up. We had brought our own transfer board with us, since Larry could not put weight on his legs at all. The left side of his wheelchair had to come off and the board then put in place. It extended from the wheelchair seat to the car seat, and he would slide himself along while I helped lift his feet into the car. It was a process. It seemed at this point in our lives everything revolved around finding ways to get through the day as easily and efficiently as possible. And truly every day we gave thanks to our Lord for giving us life, health, and strength, as well as the time we had together. In so many ways, as my husband became more dependent on me, I felt we were able to draw closer to each other and thereby experience a quality to our relationship we had never enjoyed before.

We were safely deposited at our hotel of choice at around five o'clock Saturday afternoon. We had made it! Larry was very ready for a bed to lie down on. We had chosen this hotel because it was across the street from the clinic, so I would be able to wheel him down the block and across the street every day for treatment. There would be no need to have him do the frequent transfers which were so difficult for him. It also eliminated the extra expense of daily cab fees.

The hotel had a wonderful handicap section in a separate building across the grounds and beyond the pool. A ramp took us right up to the door and upon entering the room we were impressed with its spaciousness. The bathroom, too, had a wheel-in shower. This was going to make our stay much more comfortable than anticipated.

We were all somewhat relieved to get our man settled into bed and doused with pain medication. While he slept, Shalom took a walk down the street to find some food. I stayed behind and unpacked our bags and generally tried to make our new home as comfortable as possible. After all, the plan was to live here for a few weeks at least.

Sunday morning dawned sunny, warm, and beautiful once again. Being near the end of October, I was thinking "I could get used to this!" Before Larry got up, I went out looking for breakfast and found a lovely little deli across the street. It had a mix of American and Mexican dishes readymade, as well as a good choice of cold fare, such as fresh fruits and vegetables and hard-boiled eggs, much of which was organic. It was very handy, and less expensive than eating out. It also cut out a lot of waiting time in which my husband could be resting in solitude. We made good use of the deli in the weeks to come, since our room was not equipped with a microwave. We found this somewhat strange at first, but after the treatment actually started we learned consuming microwave-prepared foods was not encouraged in pursuit of a healthy lifestyle. The entire city seemed to promote healthy living. The downtown area was blocked off every Tuesday afternoon to make way for a gigantic farmer's market where almost every stall advertised its certified organic produce.

I found out near the end of our stay that apparently Brad Pitt loved to frequent our little deli. Unfortunately, I never ran into him, and of course was much too preoccupied to care.

After breakfast and coffee in our room on Sunday, Shalom and I crossed the street to scout out another hotel. While making our first reservation, she had been told we could have our current room for only two weeks and then we would have to move out for the weekend due to a previous booking. At that time we weren't sure how long we would be staying, so we agreed to that plan. Now, however, we were planning a four-week stay and felt it would be very difficult and stressful for me to make the entire move on my own. Shalom was staying with us for only a few days and then returning home to her responsibilities. Upon seeing the room we would be booking for a weekend in the middle of our stay, we realized this was not going to work. The room was small and crowded and although we were told it was wheelchair-accessible, there was a curb just outside the room with no ramp. One step up into the room completed the picture of the impossible. I literally burst into tears as the weight of stress and care landed on me. I was altogether overwhelmed! Through my tears, I tried to explain to the attendant that this would never work for us and we would need to cancel the reservation. He kindly accepted my decision and we returned to the office of the place we were staying. Declaring and hanging onto God's promises of favour on His children, we asked the desk clerk to reconsider our need to move out for a weekend in the middle of our stay. After explaining why it was so important and how difficult it was for my husband to be moved a lot, his bones and frame being so brittle and vulnerable to injury, the young man assured us he would make other arrangements for that weekend. I cannot describe the relief I felt when this weighty issue was settled. Once again I was so thankful to God for going before us and making a way through an otherwise difficult and intimidating situation.

I was also filled with gratitude that Shalom had been able to come with us and help us get settled. She was planning to leave in three days and I missed her already. Of course, she had to keep reminding me about how I could turn on the tears so easily and get my way. We had a little chuckle over that, because I really couldn't help the tears. They seemed too near the surface during that time.

Monday morning, October 25, we wheeled Larry across the street and entered the clinic for the first time. I felt like it was my first day in grade one all over again, not knowing at all what to expect. After checking in, we were told to have a seat in the waiting area. We waited, and waited and waited. Finally I approached the desk again and explained that my husband was unable to sit for this long. I asked if they had a bed he could lie down on. I realized then that they were not well equipped to handle someone in Larry's condition. However, they did immediately spring into action trying to see what could be done to make him more comfortable. I realized in the days to come that all the other out-patients were ambulatory and, although in various stages of cancer, not one was as weak and helpless as Larry.

First the receptionist took us to a massage room to have him lie down on the table. But no, this would not work; it was too high and not adjustable. The next option was a consultation room with a recliner—a much better choice. We carefully moved him and put the chair in a reclining position.

While people were coming and going getting all our information and doing all the required paperwork, Dr. Issels himself came in and after a few questions started Larry on some natural medicines. In a short time Larry was feeling much more relaxed as the pain dissipated. The nutritionist came in and took his lunch order, as a nutritional lunch and morning snack were part of the treatment. We were verbally led through the course of any given day and introduced to the various different methods of treatment he would encounter. There were a few Larry would not be able to take advantage of. These being the oxygen chamber, which required the patient to lie down in a chest-like contraption low to the floor, and the use of the massage table. They assured us, however, that he could have a modified massage while remaining seated in his recliner. Finally they took us to the treatment room where he would be spending the majority of his time. He was assigned a reclining chair and it would become our routine to get him settled into the chair by eight o'clock every morning, Monday through Friday.

After lunch that first day, we were handed a requisition form and an address where we needed to go for a CT scan. After the scan he could go home and return the next morning when they would begin to introduce the various therapies. The trip to the lab was extra tiring for Larry, but eventually the day was over and we felt a major hurdle had been crossed successfully. Being so tired out, he settled down for a really great night's sleep. I felt that the first day, being the most stressful, was behind us and we could look forward to a smoother day tomorrow.

Santa Barbara – October 2010

The next morning we basically followed the same pattern we had set the day before: getting ready for the day, having breakfast, and wheeling down the block and across the street. This time, however, when we entered the clinic we could proceed immediately to the treatment room and settle Larry into his recliner. I must say, a tiny detail like bringing his transfer board with us was something I was immensely thankful for. It certainly made our days easier as we carried it with us wherever we went. After Shalom and I settled my husband in his place, a nurse came along and got him started on an IV line that would pump a multi-vitamin cocktail into his system. He'd had one the first morning and the result was an almost immediate feeling of increased strength and well-being. We were so encouraged by this!

Now that his day was started, I was no longer needed, so Shalom and I chose to get on the transit and look up a supermarket where I could purchase some much needed supplies, fresh fruit, vegetables, almond milk, etc. Having no stovetop or oven for meal preparation was a bit of a challenge for me, but in reality fresh foods were definitely the healthier choice. Being southern California, natural and organic produce was easy to come by. We found a Whole Foods market nearby and bought what we needed, returned to our room, and had it put away before we had to return to the clinic.

Lunch was served at noon for the patients and we were welcome to join them, for a fee. We decided to indulge in some fresh veggies instead. After lunch there was usually a lecture and discussion time and caregivers and family members were welcome and even encouraged to attend. The topics dealt with nutrition, selection and use of appropriate cleaning products and cooking utensils, the importance of positive thinking, meditation, and general frame of mind, as well as how to employ the patient's involvement in making medical treatment decisions. I personally found these lectures extremely helpful, having never walked this path before. We found it especially interesting that, on the first day they offered the lecture on mental fitness, the physician in charge of the facility suggested Larry skip the talk and go to his room for a rest. In their initial consult my faith-filled, positive husband had shared with him where his source of strength lay, and I guess the doctor felt that was sufficient. If he only knew!

We quickly fell into a routine that was comfortable for us and seemed to work well. My morning activities varied according to need—tidying our room, getting myself to a laundromat, grocery shopping, and sometimes just relaxing with a good book. As the weeks went by and I got to know several other ladies whose husbands or family members were in treatment, we would get together for coffee at the deli or go for long walks. For me, coming from the north, walking the green, flower-strewn paths of a local park in twenty-five-degree weather was a highlight. After all, it was November and I didn't need to shovel snow as I went!

In the middle of our first week there, Shalom had returned home to her job and I was left on my own with my husband who needed a lot of care. For months now I had been leaning heavily on my Lord. Larry and I had prayed through and agreed on every decision and every move we had to make. I had been focusing on finding scriptures that spoke of God's strength so readily available to us and I knew that in order to have ready access to them I should at least know where they're located in the Bible. Now was the time to draw from a well I had already filled. Not that I hadn't already been taking advantage of these promises, but the need had intensified.

I cannot fully describe the deep feelings of aloneness. Here we were, in a country not our own, totally dependent on others financially, my husband very ill, in need of constant care, and I was expected to take care of all decisions and logistics basically on my own. Other than the few people we were getting to know in the program, we didn't know a soul in the entire city. Our support group was available only by phone and we were encouraging family and friends to call on our hotel room phone to eliminate the cost for us in roaming fees.

One day we returned from the clinic in the late afternoon and were soon pleasantly surprised by a call from our daughter Berena in Winnipeg. The pleasant surprises continued as she told us she was pregnant, expecting their third child. We were so excited! We love babies at our house, so this was indeed cause for celebration. Sadly, though, this little guy, born the following July, will never get to know what a special man his grandpa was. His grandpa never got to know Zeus on this earth, so I can just imagine what a time it will be when they finally meet in Heaven!

As I mentioned, every Tuesday afternoon there was a farmer's market in downtown Santa Barbara. The streets were closed to traffic for several blocks, and tables and stations with every imaginable product were on display. I checked it out on my own first, since Larry wasn't up to the trek downtown but felt he could stay on his own for a short time. We enjoyed a lot of fresh vegetables and fruit during the weeks we were there.

During the first week at the clinic, Larry was given three multi-vitamin IV treatments. Each time he felt stronger, physically and emotionally. Each time we were more encouraged as we realized he was able to do a little more for himself. Going for a walk in the evening and seeing him wheel his own chair for a block was a big deal! We were told that in the second week my husband would be starting on a vitamin C IV infusion and they would continue three times a week as long as we remained in the program. We were warned that the vitamin C would have various side effects, as it did its work—chills and uncontrollable emotions being a few. I was thinking, "If it will help, bring it on!"

After spending a rather lonely weekend without the routine of going to the treatment centre, we were both very ready to embark on a new week of concentrated effort in health reclamation.

Joy in the Mourning

On Monday morning the vitamin C drip was started and throughout the day all the other treatments continued, all while Larry remained in his recliner. By this time, modified massage, acupuncture, and a regimen of natural supplements had been started. Several times a week we used the afternoons to go to a lab for required scans or x-rays. The vitamin IV therapies took place every Monday, Wednesday, and Friday. These proved to be long days, since the drip continued for eight hours each time.

The first day of the C-drip went well—until after supper. Shortly after the evening meal my big, strong husband melted into tears and for no apparent reason cried and cried. It took us a little while to figure out that it may have just been the reaction we had been warned about. The high concentration of vitamin C flooding his body was good, not detrimental. However, the human body is not used to such a concentrated dose. After a serious crying jag, I was on the phone calling some of our prayer supporters, then spending time reading scriptures out loud and agreeing in prayer with Larry.

Have you ever noticed how impeccable God's timing is? After praying together and committing our fragile emotional state to God, the hotel telephone rang. I answered and the voice on the other end was unfamiliar to me, but he introduced himself as David Breed from West Coast Believer's Church. I missed his explanation as to how he got our information because I was simply stunned as I heard him ask if there was anything they could do for us. Was there! I briefly explained that we were going through an extremely difficult time at the moment and I don't even remember if I asked him to come or if he offered, but within the next half-hour he was at our door. He told us that apparently Larry's sister, Linda, from Lethbridge, Alberta, had called Kenneth Copeland Ministries that day and shared our situation, asking if they knew of a church or ministry near us. They in turn got in touch with the pastor of WCBC, this church having been born out of

Santa Barbara – October 2010

their ministry. The pastor, who lived in Los Angeles where he also pastored a church, called David who lived in Santa Barbara and was a lay pastor in that church. And here he was, sent by God at the precise time of need. When I think back to that time, I just stand amazed at how God works and how timely His answers are!

After a time of sharing God's Word and praying with us, David left promising to return on Wednesday evening and bring his wife and young son with him. Now we had something to look forward to and we knew there was a connection with our family in Christ right there in that strange city. I cannot describe the feeling of the burden of aloneness being lifted from my heart, and I know my husband felt it as well. The rest of the evening passed uneventfully and that particular reaction never returned.

The next day, being Tuesday, was farmer's market day. After being dismissed from the clinic for the day, Larry said he'd like to go downtown and visit the market with me. I shouldn't have been surprised, since I could see from day to day how his strength was coming back, and his spirits were being lifted daily. Off we went, with me pushing his chair. After about five blocks, a shuttle route joined the main street and we got on when we realized they were wheelchair-accessible. After checking out all the booths and tables, we selected our fresh fruits and veggies and headed back to the hotel. Although we arrived back tired, we both agreed it had been great fun and decided we could do it again next week.

Wednesday was another vitamin C infusion, and we carefully monitored Larry's reaction but nothing out of the ordinary showed up. That evening, David Breed came for another visit and brought his lovely wife Carol Joy and his son, Max, with him. We spent our time together by the pool, so Max could enjoy a swim. Again we were so encouraged to keep standing in faith on God's word. We were beginning to feel a part of the local family of God. Of course, the next step was to connect with the rest of the family on Sunday morning. David assured us he would find a ride for us. How we looked forward to that day!

We were getting used to the routine, now. Every morning as soon as Larry was ready for the day, I would wheel him outside where he would sit, soaking up the sunshine while I prepared our breakfast and then he would eat out there. Just being in the sun seemed to strengthen him and bring down the pain level. His day consisted of the various therapies and visits with the naturopath and the onsite oncologist. Occasionally we were required to go for a lab visit, checking blood work or having an x-ray or a scan.

Every Thursday evening the clinic's nutritionist hosted a cooking class in a nearby church fellowship hall. We hadn't attended the first week, since Larry had not yet been up to it, but it was time and what an amazing time we had. Caregivers got a front-row seat so we could see it all and absorb and understand what she was doing. After she cooked, we were all served dinner amid a running commentary on the importance of nutrition, especially for a body with compromised health. I had always tried to plan meals with thought for my family's nutritional needs. However, this was a brand-new ballgame, with foods introduced that I had never heard of and could barely pronounce! But the meals were delicious and I learned a lot, and still use the knowledge I gained.

By now the first two weeks were history and half of our time there was behind us. We could see the treatments were helping, so the next step was to make plans to continue with as many facets of the therapy as possible on our return home. We began working toward that end, researching what we could do and where we could find the clinical help needed.

In the middle of all this, Sunday arrived and a dear couple picked us up for church. What an awesome service! The praise and worship was lively and God-honouring; the teaching of God's word was down to earth and practical, uplifting nourishment for the spirit-man. Many beautiful people spoke to us afterward, encouraging

Santa Barbara – October 2010

us and promising their prayers on our behalf. As I look back now, I am still nudged to pray God's blessing on this special group of people who accepted us without question, making us feel cared for when we needed it so badly. David and Carol Joy even lent us a CD player and gave us a CD of healing scriptures from Kenneth Hagin. With this CD and a couple of others featuring their pastor in his music ministry, we found our quiet evenings in the hotel room so much more peaceful.

As the days and weeks passed in Santa Barbara, Shalom was looking after things at home. All was well, except for one crisis. One morning I received a call and a panicked voice spoke quickly into the phone—so excitedly I couldn't make out what was being said. I thought Shalom was calling from a hospital emergency room reporting a car accident! After she calmed down I began to understand the true story: she opened a kitchen drawer and there, before her eyes, was a nest of tiny, pink, hairless rodents, left to helplessly stumble around while their mama made a quick escape! Oh, the trauma!

I offered my wise advice. "Call your sister-in-law. She'll know what to do."

In the end they were able to find traps and catch the adults involved, and the babies were easily apprehended. And of course, our four-year-old grandson, Austin, came to Auntie Shalom's rescue and showed her how to dispose of the ones they caught. As I said, for the most part things went smoothly at home while we were gone.

We were scheduled to fly back to Calgary on November 20 and were beginning to make plans to that end. Every day Larry spent as much time in the sun as he could. Together with all the therapies he was undergoing, we also felt his body was responding positively every time he spent an hour soaking up the warm California sunshine. A week before our return home, we finally made it to the ocean. The beach was located basically at the end of our street. That morning we had a visit from a lady in the church we had visited. She had been moved to come and minister to us, sharing God's love and spending time in prayer with us. We so appreciated that she would make the trip just to encourage us. Around noon we said we'd like to take her to lunch and she took us up on it. After enjoying a nice light lunch together, she drove us to the beach and dropped us off. It was a beautiful day and we enjoyed an almost "normal" walk along the beach till Larry began to tire and we caught a shuttle back to the hotel. After three weeks of intense focus and working toward better health, it was such a relief to take our minds off of the disease and all the pain, discomfort, and inconvenience and just be a couple spending a lovely day together.

The following week was our last there and it went by quickly. Before we knew it we were planning how to pack everything efficiently without adding too many pieces of luggage for the extra supplies and supplements we were bringing back with us.

At the end of the week, Shalom called and told me I had an appointment about two blocks from the clinic that morning. She wouldn't give any more information. I didn't know until I arrived that I was booked for an hour-long massage! What can I say? A girl knows what a girl needs.

As on the trip south, Shalom had also made all the arrangements for our trip back. All we had to do was call the cab Saturday morning and be ready when it arrived. There was a soft, warm drizzle of rain that morning, much like the first evening four weeks earlier. During the weeks we were there it never rained at all. The cab dropped us off at a predetermined spot where the shuttle bus would pick us up and transport us to LAX. When we arrived at the airport, it was just a matter of finding a luggage cart and playing "choo choo!" I can just imagine the sight we must have made—I pushing my husband in the wheelchair and he in turn pushing the cart piled so high I'm sure he couldn't see where he was going. Luckily we didn't have far to go to our check-in desk and from

Santa Barbara – October 2010

there things moved along well. Security was a breeze and before long we were headed down the jetway toward the plane. Getting Larry seated proved to be a bit of an issue in the tight quarters of an airplane, and he was slightly injured in the process. Just thinking of how brittle and fragile his bones were by this time, it was a miracle we were there at all.

We enjoyed an uneventful flight and talked about all the good things that lay before us. As Larry was so faithful in reminding me, "The best is yet to come." Landing in Calgary at minus-twenty-five-degree temperatures after leaving summer behind a few hours earlier took an immediate toll on his body. By the time we got him into the car and made the hour-long drive home, I could tell how badly he was affected by the climate change. Like the weather and the downward plunge in my husband's health, my emotions and his were ready to slide uncontrollably downward. Again the only thing we had to hang on to was our faith in a God who was watching over us and was leading us on and through, step by step. He had never yet let us down and we both knew He never would. So hanging tightly onto the rope of hope, we could say, "The best is yet to come!"

Chapter Eight
HOME AGAIN – NOVEMBER 2010

It quickly became apparent we were in for the fight of our lives when three days after returning home we found it necessary to call an ambulance and have my husband taken to the local hospital. He was suffering terribly since our return to the frigid temperatures and lack of sunshine. Some of the symptoms were back, telling us he would require another calcium flush. Above all that, he was experiencing a lot of nausea.

As the ambulance left our driveway, I followed in my car, the battle of the ages roaring in my mind with thoughts like, "Just give up, already!" Or, "He is so very ill, he would be better off in the presence of the Lord." If I am to be totally honest here, I will say these options seemed at the time to be an easy way out for me, personally. I was so tired; simply exhausted! And yet the half-hour trip to the hospital gave me the time I needed to cry out to my God once again and thank Him that He had made a way—that when Jesus went to the cross He carried our pain and infirmities, our sicknesses, and our sorrows. Being the beloved of God, the Father, I knew God had walked this road before me and He would continue to give me the strength I needed for every step. The verses espousing supernatural strength and joy I had been meditating on all summer and fall came back to me and I felt a warm, soft comforter settling on me. No wonder, when Jesus was about to ascend to Heaven He told His disciples He would go away but would be sending a "Comforter" to them. It may sound trite, but what a comfort.

Home Again – November 2010

Immediately after arriving at the hospital, Larry's blood was taken and all his levels checked and yes, he was in need of an intravenous flush, so I settled in for the hours it would take to clean out his system. During these times of waiting, I was always able to utilize the time by making phone calls to family members and friends, keeping them apprised of the situation. About this time I was informed that Larry's two older brothers were planning to drive out from Manitoba for a visit. When Larry heard that, he perked up a little and we agreed it was a good thing that this little side trip to the medical facility was taken care of for a while.

We were dismissed to leave the hospital at about 3:30 in the morning. My husband was feeling a little bit better. We needed to make only one stop on the way home, to fill a Ziploc bag with snow from the roadside because a cold pack on his thigh always seemed to help with pain control. Arriving home after four, I had to rouse Shalom for help getting her dad into the wheelchair and up the ramp. The snow and ice made it increasingly difficult for me to handle alone.

We had a good visit with Larry's brothers. It even gave me a little break. Jack was so helpful in getting Larry washed up and settled down for night. They were not able to stay with us for lack of space, but did spend most of the daytime hours at our house.

My husband's nights were becoming very broken up and Shalom and I developed a system whereby at least one of us would be available to take care of him at all times. There were days when our daughter had to start work at eight in the morning and other days when she worked a later shift. When she had the early shift, I was on night duty, and when she went to work in the afternoon she would spend the night in our room and I would try to get some sleep in her bed. It was working, but for any length of time would not have been a good solution. The hospital homecare coordinator was moving as quickly as possible to put a respite care program together for us. Larry seemed to be regressing so quickly that our plans to establish some ongoing supplemental nutrient therapies were quashed. There was just no time to work it out or to try to find necessary funding, and frequent trips to the hospital were eating up all of our time.

Very soon I got a call that we were accepted into the respite care program and were to get two hours a week in the way of "help." I hung up the phone and burst into tears. Two hours a week when I could hardly squeeze out two hours of sleep in any given night seemed like a cruel joke. Then I remembered to count my blessings. There were many! We had a good, clean hospital bed for Larry any time we needed it, God was taking care of us in every way and His provision, albeit through faithful friends and family, was always on time, never late. We had a warm, comfortable house, a dependable car, and because of insurance were not billed for the many ambulance rides he had already taken. We were so blessed to live in this country, and now to top it off I would have the opportunity to go out for two hours at least once a week and not have to worry about my husband. I immediately called my daughter-in-law, Renae, and asked if I could use that time to come and sleep at her house. And that's how I spent my very first respite visit. I was elated, and afterwards a little more rested.

The next couple of weeks, we seemed to stumble from day to day. One week, our respite worker didn't show up. A phone call revealed she was booked at the head office but hadn't received the message. Having looked forward to a short nap, it left me feeling somewhat frayed. Again, I chose to focus on the strength I knew I could get from God alone, supernatural in its very nature. It still has me in awe to think that this concept is more than a thought, much more than empty words. When I stop and breathe in deeply, taking in the peace and comfort of my Heavenly Father, it truly is as tangible as being tenderly wrapped in a warm cocoon. What a privilege to be considered His child.

Home Again – November 2010

Christmas was less than two weeks away, and we had just learned that Kerri and Berena, along with her family, would be travelling west to join us for the holiday. We were both looking forward to seeing them and Larry's spirits especially seemed buoyed by the anticipation. I was a little concerned about how they would react; so many changes had taken place since they had last seen him a few months earlier. But I knew they were strong young adults and their faith would carry them just as our faith carried us.

The homecare worker was to be at our house on Wednesday, December 15, so Shalom and I decided it was a good time to make the trip to Calgary and get a few errands done. I also planned to pick up some little gifts for the grandchildren, so we knew we would need more than two hours. Renae was kind enough to arrange to be there when the worker had to leave. In all we were gone about five hours. Just before leaving the city for the one-hour drive home, I called Renae to see how everything was going. Sadly, it had not been a good day. Larry had been sick from the time we left and was still throwing up intermittently. I was crushed and battling guilt as we rushed home. When we got there I realized my husband was a very ill man, and actually looking much sicker and weaker than he had earlier in the day. It seemed he could keep nothing down no matter what we tried. All evening we struggled with whether we should ride it out overnight and see what he might feel like the next day, or call the ambulance.

At around eleven he seemed to settle down well and became almost comfortable. I breathed a huge sigh of relief and prayed peace over him. Less than an hour later he rang for help again. We had given him a remote doorbell to summon help whenever he needed attention, since his voice was too weak to carry past the bedroom door. When I entered the room I noticed how grey his complexion had become, and his skin was slick with sweat. I called my son Scott to come over and in minutes we decided to call the ambulance. I can only recall feeling relief, knowing that at least

Joy in the Mourning

Larry would be in good hands. I honestly thought, "This is it." My thoughts were that the calcium level was too high again and maybe this time to the point of cardiac arrest.

Again I followed the ambulance in my car, thinking they would give Larry an infusion and send him back home. On arrival at the hospital he was quickly taken into emergency and in a short time the on-call doctor let me know they would keep him for observation, and in fact he was unresponsive. I did step in behind the curtain to say goodnight, but, as I had been told, there was no response. I gave him a kiss, told him I would be back in the morning, and with a heavy heart I turned and walked away, wondering if I would ever see him again on this side.

I drove home with the tears running down my cheeks and my heart crushed with a deep, deep sadness. The hopelessness of our situation stared at me through the darkness of the winter night. Arriving home in the wee hours of the morning, I tried to console myself that at least I would hopefully get a full night's sleep.

When Shalom and I got to the hospital the following morning, we stepped around the curtain in the emergency area and saw Larry lying on the cot, eyes closed, very still. A nurse approached and told us he had not been conscious since he was brought in. We spoke to him and got no response. As we stood beside his bed with me holding his hand, I prayed silently, reaffirming my faith in God for a healing miracle and asking His strength to overtake me. An incredible peace flooded my entire being and I began to imagine Christmas with the whole family together and our grandchildren running around excitedly.

Just as a smile threatened to steal across my face, the doctor came in and quietly asked if we could join him in a small meeting room. Not recognizing him, my first thought was, "Who are you anyway?" He introduced himself, explaining that he had been called in from another town because of a doctor shortage in the ER.

Home Again – November 2010

After we were seated, he explained that because of the cancer's advanced state, my husband's body was no longer responding to the calcium-flush IV treatment. They would no longer be administering that to him, and again the list of possible complications followed. Massive heart failure was near the top of the list, and Larry was already in a comatose state.

The doctor said, "Do your children all know about their father's condition?"

"Yes," I said, "I made calls last night."

"Would they be able to come quickly to the hospital?"

"Two of my daughters are in Winnipeg. They're coming in less than a week, to spend Christmas with us."

The doctor nodded sympathetically. "Ruby, I strongly suggest you call your daughters and ask them to come right away. It may be their only chance to say goodbye to their dad."

My heart slid to the bottom of my toes. Looking down at the floor, I was surprised I didn't see it quivering there. I told the doctor I would speak to my girls, so I did make a few calls back in the waiting room. I promised them I would call again later in the day, hopefully with more uplifting news.

Another member of the hospital staff came to call me into another office. She informed me that they would need to admit Larry and there were some loose ends to tie up. The social worker joined us then, and in our conversation a situation came up—actually, several experiences my husband had when he was first admitted back in September. In tears, I told the two ladies how hesitant I was to have him stay here again when he had suffered under the care of two particular staff members. He was much weaker now, both physically and emotionally, and totally unable to defend himself.

I said, "Three months ago one of them caused added injury and pain in his legs. The other one was continually harassing him with negative put-downs, basically calling him lazy and unwilling to help himself, and yes, I was there and heard him. So you can understand my hesitation now."

We came to an agreement that he would be admitted and, at my request, the two caregivers in question would never be assigned to his care.

Much later that day, Larry was taken to his room and by suppertime he was awake and alert. I called the girls with the good news and we agreed it would be best to keep the original plan. They would arrive in five days. By this time we were shifting our plans for Christmas at home to having a brief celebration in the hospital. After all, celebrating is less about location and more about spending time together.

On the morning of Sunday, December 19, we were chatting and praying intermittently when my husband's attending physician entered the room. As she began to speak, I realized she was about to say something that was difficult for her. First she commended us for our positive expressions of faith and the overall positive attitude evident in our lives. Then she told us that as a medical professional it was her responsibility to let us know the prognosis was not good. One by one, Larry's organs were shutting down, and there was nothing more they could do medically. We needed to be preparing for the last days of his life, making sure there was no business left unfinished.

As she wished us a good day and left the room, I couldn't help but wonder at the irony. No unfinished business? How about forty years' worth of unfinished business! Daughters to walk down the aisle, more grandchildren to meet and love, grandchildren to applaud on their high school and college graduations, grandkids to bless on their wedding days, and great grandkids to welcome with hugs! How about all the years of retirement that were promised to short-term missions, not to mention to me, his wife, for the sheer enjoyment of sitting side by side on the deck watching sunsets. Oh, there would definitely be unfinished business!

Home Again – November 2010

As I looked over at my husband, I saw such an incredible wash of peace and trust move across his face. It was then that I knew to the depths of my heart that we were so wrapped in the love of our Heavenly Father, there was no escape. I believe it was then that Larry came to the end of himself and just let peace carry him.

Later that day, Larry spoke to each of our children and shared what the doctor had said. The atmosphere in his room was lighter and more peaceful than it had been for a time. I'll take that!

A few days later I was sitting in Larry's hospital room wrapping the gifts we had bought for the grandchildren, then stashing them in his tiny closet. All day I had been texting with my daughters on their way west for Christmas. Needless to say, in my friend's Maritime expression, we were "some" excited! Even their dad had perked up a little as we talked and planned how we would deal with the whole family spending part of Christmas day in the hospital. The plan was that we would gather in the lounge at the end of the hall where the little ones could open their gifts, enjoy a simple lunch together, and just be together for a while. Dad and Grandpa would be in his moveable bed, which we could push the short distance down the hall. He was just too weak to even be transferred to a wheelchair.

Right around supper, Berena and Dean arrived with Max and Rambo in tow. It was so good to see them and give my girl a big hug, all the way around her pregnant tummy! I had hardly seen the little boys when they were out to see Larry in September. With his health so poor and me staying in the hospital most of the time that fall weekend, I don't recall much of seeing them. Now we had a short visit and then they headed out to our home in Cremona, a half-hour drive away. It goes without saying they were exhausted after the day-long drive from Winnipeg. About an hour later, Kerri arrived. She had driven out alone in the company of her little dog. After a brief time together, she also headed for our house. I'm sure they were rather relieved to see their dad still alert and speaking his mind.

As was my custom since my husband's return to the hospital, I spent the night in his room. The next morning Shalom arrived with Kerri and during the day we noticed that their dad was more energized and upbeat than he had been in the last week. In the back of my mind I was thinking there might be the slightest chance we could spring him out of there for Christmas at home.

That night, Kerri stayed with her dad and I was blessed with a solid night's sleep in my own bed. The next morning, I hurried to the hospital and spoke to the staff about getting a two-day pass for Larry. They were quite agreeable and started the paper process to make it possible. There was one catch: someone would have to draw and administer one of the medications. Since he had a port installed in his upper arm, anyone could learn to do it. I wasn't comfortable with the idea, so Kerri quickly volunteered and learned the procedure. She was a natural. We couldn't resist having a little fun with Scott, though, since he's so very macho and has a deathly fear of needles. We tried to convince him it was to be his job to make the injection!

We didn't tell Larry until the next day, the morning of Christmas Eve. He was doing a little better and had gained a little strength, so we were confident if he held up till the twenty-fourth he would be able to once again transfer to and from the car, chair, or bed. All went according to plan and that afternoon we picked him up and brought him home. I think he was a little apprehensive at first because he was well aware of his limitations. However, it started out well and by the time we arrived home, Berena, Dean, and the boys had moved over to Scott and Renae's in order for us to have a little more peace and quiet for Larry's sake.

Christmas Day went well and we were even blessed to have a traditional Christmas dinner, thanks to our local food bank. Someone had ordered a hamper for us and the trunk and backseat of our car were filled. It took us way past Christmas day and for that we were so grateful. God is good and always faithful!

Home Again – November 2010

It was evident Larry was being stressed to the max, and I tried to make sure he got lots of quiet time, with opportunity to nap. How can we go through a time such as this standing in faith and yet knowing it may be our last holiday together as a family? I don't know if there are any pat answers. All I can say is, truly I believe God has promised us not an absence of hardship, but His strength and faithfulness in the midst of difficulty. I also believe His promises for healing and hope for such. I believe it would be the height of arrogance to think my circumstances would change His Word. Rather I desire to see my circumstances changed *by* His Word.

The morning of Boxing Day, we had a nice big breakfast and my husband even had a second helping. I was encouraged. At lunchtime, though, he wasn't interested in food. I didn't try to convince him to eat, remembering how much he had eaten earlier. At around 3:30, we got him bundled up for the ride back to the hospital. As soon as he was settled in the car, he became very ill and lost whatever he had ingested earlier in the day. With some horror I realized it had not begun to digest in the last seven hours. My heart sank as I thought about what this meant in terms of how his body was functioning, or failing to do so. We eventually got him back to the medical facility and I believe we were all somewhat relieved. I gave a brief report to the nurse on duty and a little later Shalom and I had a short time of prayer with Larry. Leaving him with hugs and kisses, we returned to the car.

I wish I could tell you I was full of faith on the ride home, but instead Shalom and I expressed our pain and hurt to each other. We so hated to see that man we loved so much suffer like that. But after the chat with the doctor a week earlier, Larry had seemed much more at peace than he had before. Now I could only think of his favourite one-liner, "The best is yet to come!" Yes, Larry, for you!

Chapter Nine
FOREVER HOME – JANUARY 2011

Christmas was over and our daughters had returned to their respective homes in Winnipeg, while for us at home things continued in the same vein as before the holiday. Rising each morning, making the trip to the hospital, trying to coordinate the use of one car between Shalom and me, and returning home late in the evening.

Then one morning I walked into my husband's room and it was cleaned out, the bed made up in preparation for a new patient. I was informed they had moved him into a private room. Till now he had been in a double room but without a roommate. Now they were expecting a new patient and because of Larry's health status felt it was best he had a room of his own. I found him down the hall and, in spite of the pain I am sure was his constant companion, he was in a spirit of thankfulness. He expressed joy at having been able to see all of our children and grandchildren in the past week, and he was constantly telling me how thankful he was for me, his wife. It was during one of Scott's visits that he shared with us some of his wishes concerning a memorial and burial. We didn't focus on this topic for long, though, since we had had all those discussions years ago, long before we were faced with poor health.

During these last days, Larry reminded me almost every visit to be sure and remember to keep his life insurance premiums paid. Every time, I assured him I would look after it. During one of Scott's visits that week, his dad made him promise to help me continue on with the plans we had for an addition to our mobile home, as well as to help me with anything I set out to do. Getting all of these things off his chest, and receiving our promises to take care of them, seemed to bring a measure of peace to his mind.

One day we had a visit from the palliative care nurse. She thought it was time we considered having Larry moved to a hospice. Since there were several in Calgary but nothing nearer to our home, we thought long and hard about that option. In the meantime, my husband's strength was failing fast. He was totally bedridden and so fragile I needed to be extremely cautious hugging or touching him in any way. In fact, touching the bed could create enough jarring movement to cause him serious pain. This brought me to the thought that maybe a move by ambulance more than an hour away was not the answer. I brought up my concern with the nurse and together we agreed Larry should stay where he was. After all, there was a very comfortable palliative care room just down the hall. By this time the hospital staff had moved a cot into my husband's room and I was able to sleep more comfortably than in the "wannabe" recliner. However, the room was very cramped with about one foot of space between the bed and the cot. When the doctor had come to see Larry at the end of December, he was the one to ask her what was stopping them from moving him into the larger, more comfortable room down the hall. She understood very well why we did not opt for the trip to a hospice, and replied that she would order the move to the hospital's palliative care room as soon as possible. There was a stipulation, though: a family member had to stay with him twenty-four-seven. This would not be a problem, since I had been there almost full-time since before Christmas. There was no place I would rather be.

On January 1, shortly after I awoke, the doctor entered the room and informed us that Larry would be transferred down the hall the next morning. That was a mixed bag for me. It certainly meant a little more space for visitors and for me, but it seemed just a step closer to the end for my husband. Up to this time we were still praying for a miracle, and it was getting increasingly difficult to stand in faith for that. Also, Larry himself was asking us all to pray for a quick trip Home for him. If that was his desire, I wanted to support him in it. He was quite excited about being moved to the larger room and, as he expressed it, it seemed he was thinking primarily of my comfort.

This was New Year's Day and by mid-afternoon the tiny room was filled with visitors, friends and family alike. I was just looking forward to going home for the night. I really needed to have some space and be alone for a while. Shalom arrived just after supper with her friend who had driven her over. Emily, her friend, had lost her dad to cancer three years earlier and had been welcome in our home any time since we got to know her and her family. I stayed for a while, then said goodnight and left for home. Shalom was staying with her dad that night.

As I walked across the parking lot the tears began streaming down my cheeks. With the darkness accentuating my aloneness, I started driving. The snow was coming down thickly and by the time I got to the highway was beginning to swirl around the car. As fast as the snow whipped past me, the tears continued to flow till I could hardly see where I was going. A dangerous combination, I realized as I began to blot my eyes more frequently.

I cried out to God, "Lord, I don't know how to do this." Over and over I repeated that phrase through my tears and in the stillness of the car that night, peace washed over me so gently and completely as I became acutely aware of the presence of my Lord Jesus. I knew beyond the shadow of a doubt that I was *not* alone, but I was being watched over and cared for as a loving mother cares for her hurting child. What a sweet feeling; what a precious revelation! I arrived home safely and, after packing a suitcase for an indeterminate stay in the hospital, went to bed. Sleep came quickly and my rest that night was complete.

I wheeled my bag into my husband's room the next morning and not long after the staff came to move Larry to the palliative care room. It had been explained to us that once there the only item on the agenda was to keep him comfortable and as pain-free as possible. There were to be no life-saving measures taken, not even to the point of administering antibiotics. We both understood this, as did our children. Larry actually seemed a bit relieved and even light-hearted about the transfer.

Moving him and settling him into a different bed was quite the ordeal and a rather painful process for Larry. When it was completed we let him rest quietly for a time as Shalom and I made use of the private lounge across the hall. It was Sunday morning, January 2, a new year before us and neither one of us were making any plans for the months to come. How can you plan for a new year with any kind of excitement and enthusiasm when you feel as though your heart is being literally torn out of your chest? Each day is a moment by moment, hour by hour endurance. Times like that I think about how I feel a supernatural strength holding me up and I know I have that only because of Jesus. How do people go through something this traumatic without Him?

By Sunday afternoon, people were beginning to gather in Larry's room again. A sister and brother-in-law, an aunt and uncle, cousins, kids, and grandkids—we were all there to be an encouragement to a man who was *someone* to us. And here he was, so excited to be in this large, beautiful room and one step closer to Heaven! I think it hit us all at that time that he was so ready to go Home and be forever in the presence of Jesus. He led us in a short time of prayer and requested specific prayer for a speedy release from pain and suffering. Now, this may be taken as a coward's way out, but who wouldn't understand his desire if you had witnessed his agony?

One thing that became clear to me in the course of the day was that staff did not appear unless it was medication time or they were summoned. I appreciated their respect for our privacy, and since there was really nothing to be done for him anyway, I could keep watch and simply press the call button when needed.

That first night we had to learn a new routine but it caught on quickly and the nights and days seemed to float by with the only marker being yet further decline in health and strength. Every evening I would set up my cot beside my husband's bed, and during the night I slept as I had years ago with a newborn baby in the house, with one eye open and both ears attuned. At the first tiny rustle of sheets I was beside him to lend a hand, and then try to calm him and settle him down with an assuring prayer and quiet words of comfort.

When morning came the cot was moved to the other side of the room where it stayed, folded up, until needed that night. There was a private bathroom with a shower in the room and I usually had myself somewhat put together before the doctor arrived on her morning rounds. Halfway through the first week, she entered the room and quietly said for my ears alone, "I can't believe he's still with us." It hit me again: it really could be any day.

On January 4, our oldest grandchild, Zachary, celebrated his eighth birthday. It was a school day but he and his sister were allowed to skip and come to the hospital where they could "party" in Grandpa's room. But Grandpa was in no shape to party, so we moved across the hall to our own private lounge and tried to have a good time for the children's sake. It was the best we could do under the circumstances, and it was enjoyable just to have a few light moments in the midst of all the heaviness and heartache. Besides that, the cake was awesome!

My days were filled by sitting at my husband's bedside, resting my head on the mattress beside him when he was napping or just fading out as he did frequently. At times I would move to the recliner for a more comfortable position. At mealtimes when they brought his tray, I tried to help him get a little soup or yogurt into his mouth. By now he was too weak to lift his hand and feed himself. Of course, by the time the first week in palliative care was over, I was told not to feed him anymore. From here on only tiny bits of sherbet on the end of a teaspoon, or a few drops of water, were allowed. His body was shutting down and the fear was that he could easily aspirate the liquid and asphyxiate. It was the worst feeling I have ever experienced, to deny food and drink to anyone, much less the one I have pledged to love till death do us part. But the staff was adamant about that, so by January 13 all I could do was swab his mouth with water or 7 Up. Larry had always been a big man, but I could see him shrinking and fading before my eyes; and I felt so guilty. He was literally starving to death and there wasn't a thing I could do about it!

Within the second week in the "end of life" room, my husband's confusion became obvious again. He was no longer capable of speaking into the telephone when someone called. Once, he wanted to make a call on the cell phone and when I placed it in his hand he gave me a puzzled look and tried to punch in the numbers but couldn't seem to remember how. I felt so bad for him as with a crushed expression on his face he handed it back to me. Even before this he expressed several times to me how he felt almost emasculated by the fact that he no longer had control of his wallet or cell phone, or that he could no longer drive his own car. I'm not sure which was more painful to watch: his physical suffering or the emotional erosion of a strong, self-sufficient man.

On Friday, January 14, around mid-morning I was sitting beside Larry's bed watching his chest rise and fall as he slept.

Suddenly he opened his eyes and focused on me. Then, because he was too weak to move his arm, he motioned with his hand. To me it was plain, as I watched him then pat his chest with his hand, what he wanted.

I carefully lay my head down on his chest and he patted the back of my head with feather-light touches. He whispered a few words very quietly. I could not make out what he was saying, and can only guess. I assured him of my love and the fact that I would never forget him. We had in the past few months said all we thought of to say to each other, but I knew in my heart that this was the last, the final goodbye we would share. I will always carry that memory in my heart like the cherished treasure it is.

Saturday was a beautiful clear, cold, sunny day and again several people came to visit. One in particular was a gentleman who lived near us. He was a single man a bit older than we were who lived alone. A couple of years earlier, Larry had led him to the Lord and he had been coming to our house for a while the year before for supper and a short Bible study. We had grown to love him in all his gruffness and had come to recognize the marshmallow softness on the inside. It was always a joy to sit and listen to his amazing cowboy stories. Now I watched as he sat by Larry's bedside holding his hand and not even caring about the tears that dripped down his weathered cheeks.

That entire day, my husband lay, still and quiet, in a coma-like state. Noticing the effects of lack of circulation, we could tell the end was very near. The attending physician continued to pop in every morning and sometimes other times in the day, as she had time, and every time I saw her she marveled at his ability to hang on so long. I can't help but wonder if that may have been because someone was always with him and he was being spurred to hang on for us.

On Sunday, the children were there for the afternoon, and because Shalom had taken some time off from work she planned on spending the night in the hospital with us. After Scott had taken his young family home, we enjoyed quiet worship music and spoke softly with each other. Again Larry had been unconscious all day, and now we detected a distinct change in his breathing. We couldn't help but wonder if he would make it through the night.

Occasionally in the last few days a nurse would walk in and check the bag of medications he was getting. Before he had lapsed into unconsciousness, Larry had been requesting frequent increases in his pain dosages. Every time they told him, "Okay, but after this we can absolutely not give you more." And every time he was in more pain they increased it again.

Now, besides the shallow, raspy breathing, he was beginning to get restless. We prepared for a long night and began to speak to him, hoping and believing he could hear us. We prayed and encouraged him to just let go, and feel free to go be with Jesus. He said something from time to time but we couldn't understand, so we continued our vigil, talking, praying, and sometimes singing. I so much wanted him to go and escape the pain and suffering, and yet I so dreaded that final tearing apart that had to come as a result of his freedom flight. We could tell he was having a very difficult time, basically drowning.

By 4:30 in the morning, I called for a nurse for the third or fourth time and literally begged them to do something for him. I felt like screaming at them and reminding them of all the things they had told me. Towards the end, I was told, he would sleep more and more since they would be keeping the pain at bay with almost unlimited medications. Then one day in the midst of his sleep he would just slip away. I wanted to scream and stamp my foot and shout, "This is not according to plan, this is *not* what you promised me!"

I begged them to do something to relieve his suffering. They gave him another injection and shortly after that he settled down somewhat. I intended to stay by his side so he would know he was not alone, but I wanted to catch a short rest in the recliner first. Shalom got comfortable on the cot right beside her dad's bed after sneaking down the hall and getting us each a sheet from the heating cabinet. After being awake for twenty-two intense hours, I went to sleep instantly and so did my daughter. Larry was quiet and I could hear him breathing across the room.

I woke suddenly and totally two hours later. I believe it was the heavy silence in the room that woke me. I quickly got off the chair and went to my husband's bedside, and I knew. I had never seen him so still and so quiet in all the years I knew him. I wasn't so much shocked and yet a feeling washed over me that I can only describe as surreal. I felt like I was watching myself. By this time Shalom was up and we whispered, "Thank you, Jesus." At the same time, I could almost hear the sound of my heart being ripped out of me. This was what he wanted; this was what we wanted for him. So why did it hurt so much?

I tried to picture Larry as he was at that moment in the very real presence of his Lord who he loved so much and served so faithfully.

At some point I remembered to use the call button to summon a nurse or doctor. I believe they knew what they would find before they arrived. Larry's doctor was already in to make her rounds, so she entered the room and made her pronouncement. I began making calls to our pastor, our children, and siblings. I knew what had to be done and I was good at that, but I had oh so much to learn! I remembered telling God a few weeks earlier that I didn't know how to do this, and truly I didn't, but in the midst of all the pain and sorrow I knew I could count on Him to lead me every step of the way.

Eventually it was time to leave the hospital and as Shalom and I passed by the front desk I vaguely remember giving a few words of instruction to the nurse there. Then we walked out into a blustery, freezing day, but the outside temperatures were nothing compared to the deep-down coldness I felt on the inside.

For eight long months, my every waking minute had centred on caring for my sick husband. Now there were major adjustments to be made and I knew I needed to be gracious with myself and allow time to grieve but also time to rejoice. So many things had to be done, but they didn't all have to be done today. First of all, there was a real need to pace myself and allow time to get rested physically. In rest there is healing. I knew all these things in my head, but had never been called on to prove them. Now was the time. At any given time throughout the day, I would think about Larry's favourite one-liner, "The best is yet to come." And with tears coursing down my cheeks I had to say, "For you, my dear, the best has now come!"

Chapter Ten
I CHOOSE LIFE

Lord, what do I do now? This was the first question I could focus on after leaving the hospital, having said a final goodbye to my husband of thirty-five years. I knew the first week or so would be absorbed in preparation for the memorial service and spending time with family and friends. In the midst of a fog, I was able to function that first day at home as our children began to arrive, and talk of funeral plans took over most of our conversations. Of course, there were so many mixed feelings and emotions, lots of tears, and expressions of relief for the end of all suffering for our loved one.

Inside my heart there was a lot of vacillating between joy and elation as I thought of Larry and what he was doing at the moment, and giving in to the pain of separation I was feeling. It was like an intense physical pressure in my chest causing nausea to roll over me in waves. Then I would think about him in Heaven again, jumping and dancing in worship to God, catching up with all his old friends who had preceded him. Now I'm happy and relieved. And so went the first few weeks.

Our children threw themselves into preparations for the memorial service and I couldn't be more grateful. Because of their participation, there was a beautiful presentation of their dad's life set to meaningful music. In the foyer of the church, a display was set up that would fill in the gaps for people who had known Larry only in certain seasons of his life. Larry always loved to party and celebrate and of course food was a big part of it. He did enjoy good food! That became part of the celebration, too. I know every act that was done in loving memory also served to promote healing of our hurting hearts. Just spending this time with family played a big part in the healing for all of us. I know we all grieve in different ways, and yet I have to wonder how people manage when they don't have the privilege of being surrounded by family, or choose to separate themselves from family.

I know that the five stages of grief—denial, anger, bargaining, depression, and acceptance—are very real and can hit at any time, with a vengeance. Even these can be experienced to different degrees and certainly in various ordered form. I have to say, though, that even in passing through these stages I felt so cocooned, almost bubble-wrapped that I knew I was not carrying the pain alone. From childhood I have felt the very real presence of God in my life and as I grew up my faith in Him also grew.

Faith, according to Hebrews 12 in the Bible, is substance; it is evidence. With those two attributes it can be presented in a court of law and come out the winner! Faith is so much more than a mystical figment of my belief system floating around somewhere in my "aura." It is that rock-solid foundation underneath me that holds me up when the sinking sands of circumstances try to pull me down, giving way to doubt, disappointment, and discouragement. Faith is not a "leap in the dark" as some have described it. Rather, it is the assurance that, as I move forward trusting in my God to guide me, light will fall on the path ahead, causing a knowing in my very depths that all is well and I can be at peace.

My mind kept retreating to a time about fourteen months earlier when we were driving to the city of Calgary on a snowy Saturday morning. We turned off the major highway at one point and started down another highway. The snow was heavy and wet, making the road extremely slippery. Larry mentioned that he hoped we would make it up the long hill ahead on Big Hill Springs Road. There was indeed a long hill, and part of it was rather steep. As he continued to drive with his eyes glued to the road, I kept my eyes on the side of the road watching for signs. After what seemed like an eternity at slow speed, I did see the sign indicating a hill. First we had to make it down, then up the other side. As I didn't mention the sign, Larry was not aware that we had come to the huge hill. We did meet cars that were parked on the opposite side of the road, obviously not able to make it all the way up. The thick whiteness outside seemed to wrap us in a soft, white, protective cocoon.

After a few more minutes my husband said, "We should be arriving at the big hill soon." I informed him that we had just reached the bottom and were starting up the other side. He had a hard time believing me, but in a short time we saw signs that we had reached the other side. A revelation hit me then: there are times in life when God wraps us in His protection to the point where we can see only immediately ahead of us, just enough to take the next step. On a clear day we would have come to the hill and seen the valley ahead of us. This day, we were totally unaware that we were about to enter the valley, but still God kept us in a cocoon as we drove right through it and safely reached the other side. It's all in our perception. It was reinforced in me that no matter what I was to encounter in my life down the road, God would see me through. I have thought of that morning many times since.

Now I stood at a crossroad, finding it necessary to choose to wallow in my pain and grief or adopt a joy-filled, positive attitude and find the strength to move ahead and be the very best mother, grandma, sister, and friend I could be. It had become very clear to me that I was no longer a wife and therefore, after thirty-five years of being one, I would certainly need to find a new normal in my life. Having chosen the path of positive purpose, my thoughts turned to a Jeremiah 29:11, a verse that speaks of God having an amazing plan for my life, plans not to harm me, but to give me a hope and a future. Wow! That's all I needed to know.

There was always the temptation to look back and wonder, "What would have happened if…?" There were feelings of guilt to be put to rest. I should have been nicer to him when he was healthy. I should have been more understanding when he was ill. Maybe if I had done this differently, and so on. Then I found this little tidbit, I don't know who first said it, but it was what I needed at the time: "People tend to overanalyze situations sometimes, especially when someone they love dies. What-ifs aren't the solution. They are the problem." So I began to work this out in my life, choosing, when I caught my mind going there, to turn it around and instead forgive myself for not being the perfect wife. While I was at it, I thought maybe I should forgive people, especially in the medical field, that I felt could have been more clear and understanding of my husband's situation. Ultimately I also decided to forgive God; not that He did anything wrong, but in my heart and mind I needed to let Him off the hook. As Mahatma Gandhi once said, "The weak can never forgive; forgiveness is an attitude of the strong."

So I began to count my blessings and give thanks for all that I did have, rather than focusing on what, or whom, I had lost. Many years ago I had run into a friend I hadn't seen for a long time. I knew she had lost her husband suddenly about two years earlier. As I hugged her, I asked how she was doing. Her response was quick, hard and bitter. "I'm a widow! How do you think I'm doing?" At that moment I made a commitment: "Lord, if I ever find myself in that situation, I will *not* be like that." Now, the test was here. Would I sink into self-pity, or would I stand by a decision I made a long time ago? Now that I knew what it really felt like to be a widow, would I let myself burrow under the covers come morning or, by employing my faith in God, would I get up and enter my day, making my life count? After all, He has a plan for my life and a purpose for me to fulfill! Remember, the best is yet to come!

Chapter Eleven
LIVE TO WORSHIP

I can't remember a time in my life when I didn't love music. As a child and later in my teens, gospel was by far my favourite genre. I also enjoyed listening to some country, soft rock, and classical. Basically, if it was music I loved it! I also loved to sing, so when I listened I was generally belting it out as well. In the last years, my allegiance turned more to gospel, southern and contemporary, and praise and worship music. It was during the time of my husband's illness and now after his passing that I found my greatest comfort in many of the lyrics I had been giving voice to for years.

Out of my collection of favourites, my daughter Kerri pulled together a beautiful playlist of comfort set to music for Larry's memorial service. In the days, weeks, and months after the funeral, I listened to these songs over and over. Each time they brought an incredible peace to my heart as I was ushered into the presence of my Lord Jesus. Psalm 16:11 says, *"In Your presence is fullness of joy."* I depended on that truth as I depended on my next breath for life! There was no joy in anything else for a while. I still enjoyed my family, kids, and grandkids. I also enjoyed getting together with friends and so on. But it seemed these outside agents never brought the peace and joy I needed in the very core of me; the only way the depths of my spirit could really be touched was in the Holy presence of God. This is where music brought me to.

The lyrics that spoke of the love of a Heavenly Father and His care for me drove me to go deeper into His presence. There is no better way to do that than to actually spend quality time in His

Live to Worship

Word and talking to Him in prayer. I found that spilling my pain and hurt out to God cleansed my heart of much of the grief. Even when the urge was there to rail on Him for my current predicament, I knew God had big shoulders and He could handle it. It seemed that although I could get through my days, the deep gut-wrenching sadness and loneliness was lurking under my bed and slithered out and into the bed when I got in at night. Because of this, I chose to go to sleep every night with worship music playing softly.

I want to share with you some of the songs that were so meaningful to me and why I felt lifted up by the messages they portrayed. "You Are My Strength" simply expresses that when I am down and feeling hopeless, God is my strength and my hope. "You Raise Me Up" seems almost self-explanatory, since that's just what faith in Jesus Christ does! Songs like "I Bless Your Name" and "I Will Praise Him" encourage me to lift up the name of Jesus regardless of where the circumstances of life find me. "You Deliver Me" and "Amazing Grace, My Chains are Gone" express the awesome power of God in freeing me from the hold of sin and negativity of this life. My commitment to my faith was only solidified by hearing the words to "I'll Worship Only at the Feet of Jesus" and "Hold to God's Unchanging Hand." Finally, I would listen to "Look for Me at Jesus' Feet" and literally see Larry in the presence of the Lord he loved, waiting for me to join him. Releasing praise brought the presence of God and released His power, bringing victory into my life.

Victory? But my husband died. We didn't see his body healed on this earth. There were those who were asking of family members, "Do they still believe in healing?" My answer is "Yes, absolutely Yes!" God is not wrong. His word still says what it said thousands of years ago. As I stated earlier, I believe it is the height of arrogance to think that my bad day changes the course of God's word. Victory? I must conclude that the victory is in what God is able to accomplish in my heart and life as I direct my praise and worship towards Him.

Worship changed my entire outlook when I was tempted to give in to despair. I want to make it clear that music was not simply an escape for me, but rather a positive force that led me into a place where, ever so slowly, sadness and mourning was being turned into fullness of joy!

Chapter Twelve
LIVE WITH A PLAN

I've always been able to function better if I have a plan. Maybe that's because I'm just a wee bit of a control freak. How can you control something when you're not sure how it's supposed to look, or where it's going? Sickness and loss was not in the plan for my life but it came anyway, uninvited. I got through my days by planning ahead; not only did it give me something to do, but it also furnished a semblance of control which I felt I needed. Now, with my husband's passing, I needed a plan.

So many tasks demanded my immediate attention, keeping me occupied with forms to fill out, service details to arrange, and preparations to host the many family members coming. Since I had spent the past few months intensely caring for my ill loved one at home or travelling to the hospital every day, or for the last weeks living in his palliative care room, my house had been sorely neglected. Now my girls were there for a few days before the funeral and made sure the house was spit-shined and ready for company! Larry's sister, Irma, and her husband Bill flew in from Virginia and stayed at the house with the girls and me. Irma was also kind enough to take over as hostess and prepared meals when needed. I was so thankful for all the hands and all the moral support that helped me get through that first week.

After the funeral was over and everyone went back to their lives, the big question hit me: what kind of life would I go back to? What had seemed so normal a year ago was out of my grasp now. While still in the hospital and able to speak, my husband had encouraged our son, Scott, to continue the project we had started, building a sizeable addition to our mobile home. Since it was January and his work was somewhat at a standstill, Scott decided this was a great time to get the addition done. That served to keep me well occupied, with decisions to make, purchases to see to—rearranging in preparation for yet another interruption in my life. The end result was well worth it. With all this going on, I found it most effective to resort to my list-making. I do love my lists and, yes, it helps me gain that little bit of control I need in my nicely ordered life.

Looking back, I'm so thankful that Larry took care right to the end to ensure the life insurance premiums were paid. He wanted to take care of me, and I appreciate that so much. Because of his careful planning, I was able to make our home more family-friendly. As well, I could afford to live stress-free while I took time to adjust and begin to heal before searching out employment.

Every night before I went to bed, I found myself thinking through what needed to be done, prioritizing items and making a plan for the next day to tackle perhaps three or four tasks. That way I knew I could handle it and at the end of the day look at the crossed-out lines and feel accomplishment. It sounds like such a small thing, and yet the feeling of self-confidence that little achievements bring is not to be scoffed at. Often in the midst of grief, focus and concentration are sadly lacking. Following my little lists day after day kept me grounded and going forward.

About six weeks after my husband's death, some dear friends from Texas offered to fly me out for a visit—as they put it, "When the whirlwind of activity slows down and you feel you need a break." What a blessing they are! Not only did I have the privilege of spending a few weeks with them, but while I was there they took me to hear a visiting speaker by the name of Don Piper. Mr. Piper had been in a terrible car accident many years before and according to medical documentation was dead for ninety minutes. He visited Heaven and wrote a book detailing his experience, including his painful but successful recovery. The book, *90 Minutes in Heaven*, was recently been made into a major motion picture. As I heard him speak, I imagined where Larry was and what he might have been doing at that very moment. The visit to Texas was an extremely comforting time for me, and I will forever be grateful for friends who were sensitive to a specific need I had not even voiced.

I was thinking I would like to do something to leave a lasting memorial to my husband. He was a man so many people liked simply because he took the time to talk to them, say a few encouraging words, and lend a helping hand. I was reminded how before he got sick we had been planning to plant more trees in our small community; we had already spoken with a number of local residents. When he broke his femur, everything skidded to a stop. A small seed had been planted in my mind, and it grew. The final result was four trees at the end of the street where we lived. Now that I no longer live there, I know they are growing bigger each year and maybe no one else cares, but I will never forget, and one day I will be back for a visit and see them standing tall and strong like the man whose life they represent.

I began to sift through thoughts of what I would do with myself now. For so many years, my life had been determined for me simply by my role as a wife. Without that position as my guidepost, I needed to decide where my life should be going. I knew I would want to go to work somewhere, but chose to put that option on the backburner for a few months. My daughter, Berena, was expecting her third child in June, so I was happy to commit to spending a couple of months in Winnipeg helping them out. It was healing to be with family I didn't see often and especially to be available to dish out hugs and kisses to those sweet little grandsons.

My summer plans taken care of, I allowed my mind to wander into September a bit and mull through several options. One thing I did know: I was still alive and God still had a plan and a purpose for me on this earth—a purpose I had every intention of filling. By the grace of God and with His help, it will be so!

Chapter Thirteen
LIVE WITH PURPOSE

Knowing my life wasn't over propelled me forward with a mixture of feelings. One day I would be looking forward to the rest of my life and the next scared to rise from my bed in the morning, afraid to fail at life and afraid to succeed. Maybe I should say rather that my feelings shifted with the sand of moments running through an hourglass. I really had no options in the end, since life just seemed to move me forward. I did have the option of grabbing hold with white knuckles and gritted teeth or embracing and sailing on. I decided to sail.

My first task, as I stated earlier, was to prepare my home to be invaded by construction and all it brings with it. I knew that in the end it would be easier to live there and since it would create changes Larry and I had planned together, maybe it would also bring a degree of healing. Every morning I entered the day determined to be excited about what lay ahead. I knew God had awesome things in store for me and I just wanted to experience it all. I won't say I was always excited about everything I encountered as I went about my tasks, but when I felt challenged I could always look back on my commitment to live in the purpose God had set out for me when He first wrote the book on me according to Psalm 139.

After my trip to Texas in March of that year, I began looking forward to spending the summer with my daughter's family in Winnipeg. As I prepared for the drive east, I let the memories roll through my mind and began writing a list of all the places and people I wanted to see. We had lived in that city for many years and I knew memories—good and not so good, happy and sad, funny and serious—lurked around every corner. I really wanted to retrace a lot of our steps just to be there and allow myself to feel as deeply as possible—maybe laugh, maybe cry, but certainly remember. Now, I know everyone deals with grief in their own way. There is no right or wrong way to mourn, or express deep loss. I suppose if there is a wrong way to go about it, it would be denying myself and how I'm made so that whatever method I choose would not be effective and would not reflect who I am as a person. For me, embracing the memories was the right way to go. For some it may be an entire change of scenery that helps the most. To come through as a stronger, healthier person, it is important to know yourself.

One desire that has always driven me is to make a difference in someone's life. I like to think that when I leave the room, at least one person will feel better than he or she did before speaking with me. If after a conversation with me a person has to pull up his bootstraps and give it all he's got just to take the next step, I have failed sadly. I want life to look brighter and the burden of life to be lighter after sharing a few words with me. With that thought in mind, I left my home in Alberta on June 5 about the time the birds were thinking of waking up. I planned on being in Winnipeg for night, so the drive was steady, stopping only briefly as necessary.

I had been looking forward to this trip for various reasons, one of them being my love of music. All the way I had my iPod cranked to almost-max volume, belting out the songs I knew and learning the ones I didn't. The iPod was set on shuffle, so for the next thirteen hours it moved through country music, a worship song, a Christmas carol, a short teaching segment, to Southern Gospel and so on. Every few hours I was ready for silence so I could remember, reflect, and spend some time praying and meditating. Then it was back to making joyful noise! By the end of my journey that day, I was hoarse but feeling oh-so-light in my heart. I was full to the top with thankfulness and joy, and solidified in what I saw as my purpose in being there so far from home for the next two-and-a-half months.

On July 2, we welcomed into our family a tiny baby boy, Axel Zeus. The tears that threatened that day were for joy and happiness mixed with a bit of sadness that his grandpa wouldn't get a chance to cuddle and play with him, nor would Zeusie know the great man his grandpa was. But life goes on and someday they will be united in the presence of God. Ultimately that promise keeps us all going in a time of separating from loved ones.

Every day that summer I made little decisions that caused me to face my memories and experience them, forcing myself to learn to feel again. One evening I dropped in to see our former next-door neighbours. Larry had spent many summer evenings sitting around their bonfire drinking tea while they and their friends were drinking something slightly stronger and sharing joints. The gentleman had started out being quite sarcastic about the fact that we were "religious" and did nothing but attend prayer meetings. They slowly thawed and before long realized we were normal people. As Larry's prayers went before God on their behalf, and our love went out to them every chance we had, we became welcome at their weekly bonfires. The last time we saw them before moving west, Larry challenged him with an invitation.

"If we never meet again on this earth, make sure we'll meet in Heaven."

The neighbour replied, "I'll do my damndest."

That was good for enough for us! Now, I had to see them and let them know of Larry's passing. Amid shock and tears, I felt their love for my husband and for our family and me. It was a healing time.

I decided it was time to visit our local golf course one evening, and as I walked around the pro shop and the grounds, the dam inside of me started to crumble. The ache in my chest was so intense it brought the old familiar nausea and the buckets of tears. Through the tears, a smile slowly emerged like a rainbow as I remembered the time Larry took me there for one of our regular evening dates to teach me how to play golf. It was only my second time golfing, and by the time we got to the eighth hole it was dark. I won the game and I would never let him forget it!

In Larry's career as a cabinet installer, he spent a lot of time working in Kenora, Ontario. Quite often I was able to accompany him on these trips. It usually meant being away from our growing children for at least two days, sometimes three. One warm Saturday in the middle of July, my daughter Kerri and I decided a road trip was in order. We headed east to Kenora. It was just a quick jaunt, a picnic in the park and then back to Winnipeg, but taking the time to feel the mix of joy and sadness and saying goodbye to those memories was so important in light of my choice to live my life on purpose.

I've lived long enough to realize that unless I do things on purpose to reach a certain goal, I'm living in vain. One cannot expect to let life happen by accident and still meet a worthy goal. In this case, my purpose was to push through the pain of grief and loss rather than run from it. In running, it might have seemed I was leaving the loss behind, but it would eventually catch up with me at a time not of my choosing, when life forced me to slow down—which it always does. Rather than have it suddenly pounce on me when I'm unaware, I would rather be prepared. Maybe that's my controlling nature showing up; so be it.

At the end of the summer, I travelled back into the setting sun, feeling that in some small way I was prepared to continue on by myself. I felt I had accomplished something and come a little way on the road to complete healing. Certainly I could see now that God still had an awesome purpose for me to fulfill and I was committed to waking each day to walk out that day's purpose in all the little things God would lead me into. Those little things make up the big picture I will only see in its completeness when I get to the end of my journey. In the meantime, I'm excited about what's ahead and what I have yet to do to complete my purpose!

Chapter Fourteen
LIVE REACHING OUT

As I neared the Alberta border on my drive west that warm Sunday afternoon near the end of August, it began to hit me that I was about to arrive at home. The home Larry and I had given much thought to and planned lovingly to share for many years. There was a catch; I was going to have to live there and carry on alone. The pain began to press heavily on my chest and a lot of tears were shed as I drove along deeply in thought. The nearer I got to my home, the more real the feelings of dread became. I dreaded walking in and unpacking, knowing I would have no one to share my home with. In fact to even think of it as home now seemed a stretch. All my life I'd had people around me. Even as a young single adult I never lived on my own, but with friends and roommates. I heard the quiet voice of my Lord inside my heart assuring me of His presence and His promise that He would never leave me.

Buoyed somewhat with the promises of God, I entered my house and took a walk around. Scott had completed the renovations while I was gone, and I was pleasantly surprised with how nice and new everything looked. The workmanship was excellent, and of course I expected no less from my own son! Kerri had travelled, in caravan, back to Alberta with me. She was planning to stay a week and then head home to Winnipeg. It was really good to have her there as I settled into the newly expanded house. It helped to cushion the sudden transition, and we had a great time going for long drives in the country, antique shopping, and just hanging out together.

Live Reaching Out

I never realized how extremely loud silence can be until Kerri left and I was left alone. The larger space echoed as I walked about doing my little daily tasks. My one consolation was that I had three grandchildren living a few doors away. I was sure they would happily comply should I decide I needed a little noise around the place!

As soon as I was settled in I contacted my friend, Cathy. We had spoken on the phone when I was still in Manitoba and she mentioned her daughter was looking for a respite worker to help out with her autistic son. Cathy had asked if I would be interested in working with ten-year-old Noah about fifteen hours a week. Having had a lifetime working with children, several of them with various challenges and handicaps, I was very interested. As it turned out, I was chosen to be Noah's respite worker. Oh, Noah! I could write a book on that boy alone. What a delightful child; every moment with him was a bucket of laughs. We loved to drive down the road and listen to my music and of course sing along. Or rather, I sang and he laughed at me. He did eventually start singing along, too. We had a lot of fun together.

Since Larry's passing, I had thought a lot about what I would do for meaningful work. Since I had been a stay-at-home mom for our four children and then run a home daycare for over twenty-two years, I knew I loved to work with people rather than machines, paper, or numbers. I had also set myself a goal to start working in September, so now it was the beginning of that month and the most amazing job had fallen into my lap. As much as I enjoyed spending time with Noah, it was my desire to work at least twenty hours more per week. It seemed the thought had barely sunk into my brain when I was made aware of a need for a nanny in my area. I called immediately and left a message. It was several days before I got the return call, and as it turned out a mini telephone interview. It sounded very promising and I began to pray that God would lead me in the right direction regarding the position. We met in person a few days later for a real interview, and it was love at first sight for me. The little boys were one and four and so sweet. The parents were extremely likeable and easy to talk to. They were looking for in-home help for about twenty hours a week. I knew this was where I needed to be and I prayed that if they offered me the job I would be able to fill a unique need in their home for as long as they needed me. I stayed with them for three years and left only when the boys outgrew their need for a nanny as school had taken my place. I only hope that I filled the gap for them as they did for me. The one major thing I learned in their home was that in reaching out and giving unreservedly of myself, so much more was given back and my life became so much richer.

Sadly, six months after I started working with Noah, his mom decided to move back to the Maritimes, her former home. I missed him, but knew there were other things in store for me. Because it was the middle of a cold, snowy winter, I was quite content to leave pursuit of another job until the weather was more pleasant. Also, I had a few trips in mind for spring and early summer, so I felt the timing was just not right to go that direction.

In July, I was reading the paper and came across an ad for help needed in a local care home. One résumé, phone call, and interview later I found myself walking the corridors of a care centre where I grew to love the residents and most of the staff in the two years I worked there. Being on the cleaning staff, I spent a lot of time in the tiny apartments and rooms of the people in the assisted living wings. Those dear seniors taught me so much and I cannot help but applaud them when I think of the lives they built in the process of building this country of ours.

One particular gentleman, Ray, was quite gruff on the surface, but I always felt he was a softie on the inside. He made a point of telling me often how he felt about "religion." And it wasn't good. Just before Easter, the decorator set up a display in the entrance hallway. It was a beautiful rugged cross resting on a table with an open Bible leaning against it.

As I met him in the hallway, he gave me a look of disgust and said, "They've got a *Bible* on there."

I just smiled at him and said, "That's okay, I read mine every day."

He stopped and looked at me for a few moments and in a voice of wonder said, "That's why you're so pure."

I knew that I wasn't so pure, but what he was expressing was an acknowledgment of the spirit of Jesus Christ evident in the way I lived my life. Forever after that he was my greatest champion, always letting me know of the great reviews he gave me in their staff/resident meetings. I have since moved away from the area and that job, but whenever I make the trip back to the Calgary area I try to visit my friends at the care centre. Many have passed on, but I pray that in reaching out and giving a little above and beyond, maybe I touched someone's life and made a difference. As for Ray, I make sure I stop by and help him find a few of those always-elusive puzzle pieces.

My desire is to work hard at emptying my life into the lives of others, because I've discovered a little secret. It's impossible to empty my life for others because it just keeps coming back in spades and filling me back up to overflowing. I am convinced that is the way to live life if you want true happiness and you want to look to the future with a sense of anticipation and excitement.

Chapter Fifteen
LIVE TO BLESS

When you're body-slammed with a tragic event such as the loss of financial security, losing your home, or the death of a loved one, it's extremely difficult to lift your eyes above the situation. So many mornings I was tempted to simply pull the covers up higher, close my eyes again, and wish the world away.

However, having lived in the promises of God for years, I knew there was a better way of dealing with pain. A while ago, I was in church Sunday morning listening to a sermon being presented by a young man who often spoke in the pastor's absence. This speaker was not a pastor—he's not a member of the church staff—but he is gifted and committed to God. He has an interesting, lively, almost comedic way of expressing godly truths and challenging a response. His topic this day was "Cure for the Common Existence."

What stood out to me the most in the sermon was that God has a wonderful purpose for me to be here on this earth. First and foremost in this purpose is to be in relationship with Him. He has laid out a big-picture outline, which He wants me to complete and fill in the sub-points. God created in me a brain that is capable of planning and carrying out good works, and He has even prepared those good works for me to do, according to Ephesians 3:10. Not only that, but He has equipped me with the gifts and abilities to accomplish those good works. But there's more: He has also qualified me by adopting me and making me His child, and given me all the authority that goes along with being a child of the Living

God. When life is trying to wrestle me to the ground, I try to remember that.

One of my former pastors stated more than once, "If you're depressed, bake some cookies and give them away!" My interpretation of that advice is that no matter how bad my situation seems, there is always someone in worse shape. When I lift my eyes off myself and look around, God will show me who needs a touch from Him. It's my job to be obedient. As Mother Teresa has so beautifully put it, "We ourselves feel that what we are doing is just a drop in the ocean, but the ocean would be less because of that missing drop."

Have you ever peeled an onion? It's been known to bring a few tears. There came a point when I began to feel the pain stripping away one layer at a time, bringing with it torrents of tears. Shortly after my husband's death I had a deep, gut-wrenching crying jag. I looked out my window and saw one of the most spectacular sunsets, and the tears came. I cried deeply as I remembered how we used to joke about sitting on the deck and watching the sunsets together in our retirement years. And in all honesty, I had never seen the quality and absolutely perfect beauty of that sunset in any location we had lived before. Sometime later, as I was wiping my tears and cooling my face, I realized how much lighter I felt. It was cleansing and it was healing.

Months later as I was relaying this incident to my niece, she asked me, "So how is it going today? Are you 'Beyond the Sunset' now?"

It took many more sunsets, many more family get-togethers, and many more little memories and moments stripping away layers of peel. Always, after letting go of a little more grief, joy and peace came to replace the pain and there was more room for blessing to grow and overflow.

Looking back today, I'm not even sure the onion is completely peeled. Certain things will still set off a few tears, even though my life is now completely different. Writing and revisiting every day of those months and years, reliving the pain and loss and touching the grief again, has shown me that complete healing is a lifetime process. I guess what I really want to say is, let the pain slip off one peel at a time, count your blessings, and determine to reach out to someone else. It will start you on a road that will take you places you've never imagined. It won't happen in a day, but be kind to yourself, be patient with yourself. It is a process, a journey you will enjoy traveling and someday when you get to the end you will hear your creator say, "Well done. Whatever you did for others, you did for me. My child, you are blessed!"

Beware of going through life with your eyes on the rearview mirror. Give it brief, passing glances—long enough to cherish the memories, remember a lesson learned or a blessing received or a challenge to aspire to. To live looking back is as dangerous as driving with your eyes constantly focused behind you. You miss the all-important signs that tell you where you need to be headed. You forget to give God thanks for daily blessings He showers on you. Most importantly, you forget how to be a blessing to those around you: loved ones who look to you for guidance and encouragement, or friends who need to see your smile and hear your light-hearted laughter.

How do I continue and move beyond mere existence into a meaningful life? Where do I find the peace that passes understanding? How do I find the oil of joy in the midst of the ashes of mourning? As the Booth Brothers end the beautiful song, *In Christ Alone*, "My Comforter, my all in all...My source of strength, my source of hope, is Christ alone!"

Scriptures

The path through deep sadness, heartache, and loss would have ended very differently had it not been for the promises in God's word. I clung to them like a drowning person holds on to the life-saving ring. I could not afford to go a day without reading and appropriating all that they stand for. This is not an exhaustive list, but only a few that helped propel me through some very difficult days.

God's Faithfulness:
Lamentations 3:22–26

God's Strength and Deliverance:
Exodus 15:2
Deuteronomy 33:25
1Chronicles 16:11
Nehemiah 8:10
Psalm 18:1–2
Psalm 27:1
Psalm 29:11
Psalm 46:1
Psalm 68:35
Psalm 71:16
Psalm 81:1
Isaiah 30:15a
Isaiah 40:29–31
Jeremiah 16:19a
Habakkuk 3:19
2 Corinthians 12:9
Ephesians 3:16
Philippians 4:13
2 Timothy 4:17–18

God's Plan and Purpose:
Jeremiah 18:1–4
Jeremiah 29:11–13

God's Joy:
Nehemiah 8:10
Psalm 16:11
Psalm 30:5b
Jeremiah 31:13
Galatians 5:22
1 John 1:4

Epilogue

You may be asking, "Where are you now in your journey? What is your life like today?" I'm so glad you asked! Let me tell you.

At the time of writing, it has been five years since my husband's passing. There are still times when a memory will cause a few tears or there will be a momentary regret for all the things I didn't do right in our marriage; for the times I could have been more understanding when he was ill. I don't know if those thoughts will ever be forever in the past. But as each layer is removed, new healing takes place and life moves on.

Before the first year was up, I knew that when the time was right I would be ready to love again if I met someone who shared my values and interests. I just determined to live my life and walk in joy and victory and not worry about that part.

Sometime later, I decided to step out on a limb and register on an online dating site. After meeting a few toads, the prince came along. The more I got to know him, the more interested I became. I guess he felt the same way, because about a year after we met we were married in the lovely little chapel of the care home where I was working at the time. The attendees were our family of four children each, their spouses, and a total of eighteen grandchildren. It was a party!

It was necessary for me to relocate to a town northeast of Edmonton because of my husband's work. It has been good. Making new friends and trying to fit into a new community and church has provided some challenges, all worthwhile.

If you have travelled this road with me, let me tell you, "There is hope!" You are not alone: *"… weeping may endure for a night, but joy comes in the morning"* (Psalm 30:5).

To contact the author, email her at
rubywiebe52@gmail.com